Group Project Student Role Sheets

Everything You Need for Successful Group Research Projects–Start to Finish!

Written by Christine Boardman Moen

Illustrated by David Helton

Teaching & Learning Company

1204 Buchanan St., P.O. Box 10
Carthage, IL 62321-0010

This book belongs to

_____

Dedication

This book is lovingly dedicated to my husband, Tom.

Cover art by David Helton

Copyright © 1999, Christine Boardman Moen

ISBN No. 1-57310-199-0

Printing No. 987654321

Teaching & Learning Company
1204 Buchanan St., P.O. Box 10
Carthage, IL 62321-0010

Table of Contents

Dear Teacher or Parent,

We teachers love success. We celebrate the achievements of our students, and we talk excitedly to other teachers—and whoever else will listen—about the great things happening in our classrooms.

At the same time, we teachers know that the road to successful teaching and student learning is paved with a lot of planning, preparing and ultimately reflecting.

As I reflected on my efforts over the past several years to move my classroom from a teacher-centered classroom to a student-centered classroom, I realized that one of the teaching-learning strategies that played a significant part in this transformation was the classroom group research project.

I have been fortunate enough to do classroom group research projects at different grade levels across different content areas. Consequently, I have had the opportunity to reflect on the entire group research project process and carefully select what worked and discard what didn't work. This book is the result of that careful reflecting-selecting process.

The most significant feature of this book is the use of individual student roles within the cooperative group project setting. The use of student roles allows students to be held individually responsible for part of the research that must, in turn, be integrated with other students' research to create a group project presentation. This cooperative yet individualistic approach allows for individual as well as group success.

Taken entirely, this book will help you implement group research projects in your classroom. Based on a respected group investigation cooperative learning model, this book includes reproducible student role sheets and group presentation strategies that establish an easy-to-follow group research process and project framework. In addition, ready-made rubrics and checklists allow for student and teacher assessment at nearly every step during the project. In other words, the book is designed to provide everything you will need for successful group projects—from start to finish!

However, if you don't want to go from start to finish—and many teachers and students have their own ideas and needs—this book can be viewed as three-books-in-one. If you decide you and your students are the "three-books-in-one" types, you may want to use only the Information Gathering Roles with different classroom projects or separate the Information Processing and Organizing Roles to use with a variety of classroom activities. The Information Presenting Roles can be used with a wide assortment of content areas and group sizes while being especially useful while planning activities based on the Theory of Multiple Intelligences.

Before you take the plunge into the arena of classroom group research projects, carefully read the introductory materials and the explanation of the step-by-step process approach. Then start planning and preparing not only for your group projects but also for the great successes we teachers love!

Happy, happy teaching!

Christine Boardman Moen

The Purpose of This Book

This book is designed to help the student research groups in your classroom

- generate a list of relevant topics and subtopics for research
- plan and conduct research using a variety of resources
- process and organize research information
- plan and carry out a group research presentation
- assist in the evaluation of the group research process

By using the materials in this book, your student research groups will be able to stay focused, meet deadlines and complete their required assignments. Using a respected model of group investigation as a guide, this book provides all the materials you will need for successful group projects–from start to finish!

With its reproducible student role sheets and group presentation strategies, the materials in this book establish a process and a framework to guide your students through the stages of gathering, organizing and presenting information. In addition, ready-made assessment rubrics and checklists allow for easy evaluation by you and your students.

Using a Group Investigation Model as a Guide

The group investigation model includes six stages: determining the topic, planning the investigation, carrying out the investigation, planning group presentations, making the presentations and evaluating the projects. The information in this book breaks these six stages of the group investigation model into 10 easy-to-follow steps that are based on students utilizing three categories of student research roles:

Information Gathering Roles

These roles enable individual students to utilize a variety of resource materials in order to gather information about their specific group research topic.

Information Processing and Organizing Roles

These roles enable individual students to utilize a variety of information organizers as they process and organize their research information for understanding.

Information Presenting Roles

These roles enable individual students to integrate their research information with other group members' information to create a group project for presentation to the entire class.

The Purpose of Student Research Roles

The use of student roles in a group research project allows students to work cooperatively to produce a group presentation yet be held individually responsible for part of the research. This individual effort and responsibility focused toward the creation of a group research project may fall into what Johnson and Johnson in *Learning Together & Alone* (Prentice Hall, 1987) call "an ideal teaching situation (which) is to assign a cooperative project and provide individual tasks for various aspects of the problem so that different group members can master different skills and information for later integration into the group's product." (p. 19). Thus this cooperative yet individualist approach to learning can be achieved by students completing individual research role responsibility sheets that are then used to create an interdependent final group project.

Students working cooperatively yet independently is what Johnson and Johnson (in the work cited above) call positive interdependence which " . . . promotes a situation in which individuals work together in small groups to maximize the learning of all members, sharing their resources, providing mutual support, and celebrating their joint success." (pp. 125-126).

In addition to promoting positive interdependence, using student role sheets in the group research project setting promotes individual accountability, which " . . . increases individual participation and aids in equalizing participation, and eliminates the problems of the freeloader and the workhorse" according to Spencer Kagan in *Cooperative Learning* (Kagan Cooperative Learning, 1992, p. 15:2).

Consequently, the student research role sheets allow students to act individually and assume responsibility while at the same time requiring the student to use this information as part of the whole group presentation.

Recognizing the Cooperative Learning Component

In *Cooperative Learning in the Elementary Classroom* (NEA Publications, 1993) Lyman, Foyle and Azwell state " . . . cooperative learning brings together the cognitive domain (knowledge) and the affective domain (feelings) within groups of interacting students. The cognitive question, 'Do I have the necessary information?' is balanced with the affective question, 'Have I listened to the information?' " (p. 15)

In addition to bringing the cognitive and affective domains together, research has shown that cooperative learning produces such positive outcomes as the following:

- increased racial and gender tolerance and friendship (Johnson and Johnson, 1981)
- increased problem-solving abilities (Johnson, Skon and Johnson, 1980)
- increased comprehension, recall and transfer (Humphreys, Johnson and Johnson, 1982)
- increased self-esteem (Johnson, Johnson and Rynders, 1981)

Using student research groups in your classroom assumes that you will be using cooperative learning strategies such as encouraging everyone to participate, not allowing students to "put down" one another, and gathering into groups in an orderly fashion. However, teaching social cooperative learning behavior is beyond the scope of this book. Some excellent cooperative learning resources include the following:

Johnson, Johnson and Holubec. *Cooperation in the Classroom*, 1990.

Kagan, Spencer. *Cooperative Learning*, 1992.

Slavin, Robert. *Cooperative Learning: Theory, Research, and Practice*, 1990.

The 10 Steps in the Group Research Process

Below is the list of the 10 steps used in the group research process. You will want not only to read this list but also to read thoroughly the explanation of how to implement each step before proceeding with your own classroom projects.

Step 1

Students and teacher generate a list of research topics based on interest, available resources and connections to the curriculum. Topics are examined for subtopics and attributes.

Step 2

Teacher decides how to form student groups based on selected criteria.

Step 3

Student groups engage in a planning session where they choose a topic, decide on Information Gathering Roles and specify deadlines.

- Assessment rubric/checklist available for student and teacher evaluation of Step 3

Step 4

Students conduct research utilizing Information Gathering Roles.

- Assessment rubric/checklist available for student and teacher evaluation of Step 4

Step 5

Students take their completed role sheets to the group's sharing session where they share information and available resources about the topic. Students select graphic organizers from the Information Processing and Organizing Roles.

- Assessment rubric/checklist available for student and teacher evaluation of Step 5

Step 6

Students process and organize information using graphic organizers.

- Assessment rubric/checklist available for student and teacher evaluation of Step 6

Step 7

Student groups meet in a preparing session where they discuss their research information, assess group talents, choose a group presentation role, divide up responsibilities and specify a presentation date.

- Assessment rubric/checklist available for student and teacher evaluation of Steps 7 and 8

Step 8

Groups complete the preparations for their presentations.

- Assessment rubric/checklist available for student and teacher evaluation of Steps 7 and 8

Step 9

Groups complete their presentations for the entire class.

- Assessment rubric available for teacher evaluation of Step 9

Step 10

Students complete a final assessment of the entire research project experience.

- Response sheet available for student evaluation and teacher reflection

Tips for Getting Started

Before beginning your classroom group research projects, it's important that students have an overview of the entire process. This will give students a sense of where they're going and what will be expected of them during the course of the project.

To begin, give each student a list of the 10-step process and briefly explain each step. (A reproducible list of the 10 steps can be found on page 11.) Next, have students staple or tape the list onto the cover of a paper two-pocket folder. (The folder should also have rings that can hold loose-leaf paper.) Explain that the folder must be with the student in class every day and that all handouts, notes, calendars and research information go into the folder. Using only one folder will help students stay organized.

Finally, post a larger-sized list of the 10 steps in the classroom as a reminder. At this time, don't go into due dates, group members or any specific details. At this point, it's important that students have an overall understanding of what the project and process will involve and how they can stay organized.

Troubleshooting Tips

For the most part, being organized and optimistic will ensure smooth running of your classroom group research project. For those times when things don't go quite so smoothly, following is some advice on what to do about students who are absent, students who are uncooperative and students who do not complete their required roles.

Students Who Are Absent

Students who are occasionally absent will not impede the progress of the group's project since the project will take place over an extended period of time. Occasional absences can be dealt with by rescheduling a group session if necessary or requiring the student to complete his or her role responsibilities as part of his or her work.

If you have a scheduled group evaluation and a group member is absent, you may want to evaluate another group or proceed with the group evaluation anyway and try to do another group evaluation a second time when all members are present. However, if you complete a group evaluation when a students is absent, make sure you do not use the evaluation when computing the absent student's grade.

Students who are chronically absent or who are absent for an extended period of time, may impede the progress of the group and should be dealt with differently. If you are aware of a student's chronic absences, you may want to put him or her as a fifth or sixth member in a group. This way, the group is still large enough to continue its project and compensate for the absent student. At the same time, he or she is able to contribute when he or she is present.

Students who have been absent for an extended period of time or who plan to be absent for an extended period of time during the project need to be treated on an individual basis. If a student is returning to school or leaving school because of an illness, injury or family situation, you may decide what's best for that particular student. Talk to group members before the student returns or leaves and decide if the student's part in the research project can be altered. In this way, the student can still be a part of the group and the group can still count on the student's contribution, but the student is not overburdened and the group's progress is not impeded.

Students Who Are Uncooperative

Getting an uncooperative student to cooperate often takes a combination of planning and prevention. Some strategies to assist you with an uncooperative student include:

- allowing the uncooperative student to work with a partner instead of a group

- assigning the uncooperative student to a group comprised of students with whom the student wants to work and who are willing to work with the student

- creating a list of unacceptable behaviors and reviewing the list of behaviors with the student and group members before each group session

- requiring the uncooperative student to work on collaborative skills with a social worker, special education teacher or counselor outside of class

However, if an uncooperative student's persistent bad behavior begins to seriously jeopardize the entire group's efforts, then the student should be removed from the opportunity of being part of the group process and given an alternative assignment. However, if you remove a student from a classroom group research project once, the student should be allowed the opportunity to participate the next time you set up a group research project. At the same time, the student should be aware that he or she will be removed once again for disruptive behavior.

Students Who Do Not Complete Their Required Roles

Conscientious students will, of course, complete their required roles and be valuable assets to their groups. Students who are not quite so conscientious sometimes benefit from being in group situations because other group members prod them into completing their work.

Sometimes students do not complete their assigned roles because they are unsure of what to do or are so disorganized, they fail to complete their role in a timely manner. These students benefit from being in group situations because they are around other students who are completing similiar tasks and who are modeling good organizational skills.

If you are aware that a student may have difficulty or be unwilling to assume his or her role responsibilities thereby impeding the group's progress, you may want to consider employing the following strategy.

Okay . . . why isn't this done?

First,
- determine if the student is not completing his or her task as a result of lack of understanding, lack of organization or unwillingness. Ask the student to explain in his or her own words what his or her role is and how to complete it. Also, you may want to encourage the student to work with a student from another group who is completing the same research role. Since each student is working on a different topic, neither can copy; however, the stronger student can serve as a model for the other student.

Next,
- establish a daily contract with the student and have him initial the tasks he or she is to perform each day. The following day, check for task completion.

Also,
- document due dates using a calendar. Keep one calendar for yourself and one calendar attached to the inside of the student's project folder.

Finally,
- reinforce the idea that every student role is essential for group success.

Since most of the project work is done during class time, you should be able to monitor a student who may have difficulty getting his or her work done. However, a student who, after your best efforts, remains *unwilling* to complete his or her work should be removed from the group. The student should be given a failing grade for the group project and be required to complete an alternative assignment.

As with the uncooperative student, the unwilling student should be allowed to participate the next time you set up a classroom group research project. Like the uncooperative student, the unwilling student should be aware of the consequences of his or her refusal to complete role responsibilities.

Ten Steps to Successful Group Research Projects

Group Investigation in particular encourages students' initiative and responsibility for their work, as individuals, as members of study groups, and as members of an entire class.

Sharan & Sharan
Cooperative Learning in Social Studies

Step 1

Students and teacher generate a list of research topics based on interest, available resources and connections to the curriculum. Topics are examined for subtopics and attributes.

Step 2

Teacher decides how to form student groups based on selected criteria.

Step 3

Student groups engage in a planning session where they choose a topic, decide on Information Gathering Roles and specify deadlines. Students and teacher may assess.

Step 4

Students conduct research utilizing Information Gathering Roles. Students and teacher may assess.

Step 5

Students take their completed role sheets to the group's planning session where they share information and available resources about the topic. Students select graphic organizers from the Information Processing and Organizing Roles. Students and teacher may assess.

Step 6

Students process and organize information using graphic organizers. Students and teacher may assess.

Step 7

Student groups meet in a preparing session where they discuss their research information, assess group talents, choose a group presentation role, divide up responsibilities and specify a presentation date. Students and teacher may assess.

Step 8

Groups complete the preparations for their presentations. Students and teacher may assess.

Step 9

Groups complete their presentations for the entire class. Teacher assesses.

Step 10

Students complete a final assessment of the entire research project experience.

Step 1

Students and teacher generate a list of research topics based on interest, available resources and connections to the curriculum. Topics are examined for subtopics and attributes.

Think-Pair-Share

When it's time to create a list of possible research topics, it's important that you and your students generate as many topics as possible without any positive or negative feedback about the topic suggestions. This brainstorming session can help produce a topic list far longer and more interesting than any list you could produce alone or get from a textbook.

One way to help facilitate a list making session is to begin by using the Think-Pair-Share method (Lyman, 1987) before you open the session to random suggestions. First, students think of topics on their own. Next, they share their topic suggestions with another student. The pairs refine and expand their list. Finally, student pairs share their suggestions with the entire group and their ideas are put on a master topic list.

Topic Evaluation Sheet

The next step is to evaluate the suggested topics based on the level of student interest, the amount of available research resources and how the topic is or can be related to what students are currently studying.

Using the Topic Evaluation Sheet on page 13, you can choose to do this step yourself. First, ask your students to tell you their level of interest in each topic and record their responses on the sheet. Next, with sheet in hand, ask your librarian to identify which topics can be readily researched in the library. Finally, determine each topic's connection to your curriculum.

However, working together with your students to evaluate topics will not only help generate enthusiasm for your classroom research projects but also allow your students to begin viewing themselves as researchers.

First, create an overhead transparency of the Topic Evaluation Sheet that has the topic sug-

gestions written in the left-hand column. As you discuss the list, record the level of student interest for each topic. Next, ask students to tell you what they think the connections are between each topic and content area. Refine and expand on their connections. Finally, assign topics to groups of students and do a "library sweep." Set a time limit and have student groups go through the library and list as many resources as they can find that pertain to their assigned topics. Return to class and complete the "Resources Available" column of the Topic Evaluation Sheet. (Inform your librarian or media specialist when you plan to do your "sweep"!)

Topic Breakout Sheet

Once the topics have been evaluated based on interest, available resources and curriculum connections, you may decide the preliminary final list of topics, allow your students to decide the list or do a combination of both.

However, this "final" list is only a preliminary list because the topics that survive the Topic Evaluation Sheet review must be broken into subtopics. Consequently, the final step in creating the final topic list is for you and your students to complete the Topic Breakout Sheet on page 17. By completing a breakout sheet for each topic area, you and your students will not only discover and discard topics that are either too broad or too narrow, but you will also be creating some of the information student groups will need during their planning session in Step 3. (Sample Topic Breakout Sheets are available for your review on pages 14-16.)

Finally, when considering topics and subtopics, it's important to note that older student groups are more capable of researching one entire subtopic with all its attributes while younger student groups will do better if their research is limited to one attribute from one specific subtopic.

Once the breakout sheets are completed, the remaining tasks in Step 1 include creating the final topic list, distributing copies of the list to students and posting the list in the classroom. (Keep the breakout sheets for later!)

Topic Evaluation Sheet

Topic	Resources Available	Student Interest	Curriculum Connection	
	Abundant Adequate Minimal	Yes No Somewhat	Lang. Arts Geography Soc. St./ History	Math Science Music/Art
	Abundant Adequate Minimal	Yes No Somewhat	Lang. Arts Geography Soc. St./ History	Math Science Music/Art
	Abundant Adequate Minimal	Yes No Somewhat	Lang. Arts Geography Soc. St./ History	Math Science Music/Art
	Abundant Adequate Minimal	Yes No Somewhat	Lang. Arts Geography Soc. St./ History	Math Science Music/Art
	Abundant Adequate Minimal	Yes No Somewhat	Lang. Arts Geography Soc. St./ History	Math Science Music/Art
	Abundant Adequate Minimal	Yes No Somewhat	Lang. Arts Geography Soc. St./ History	Math Science Music/Art
	Abundant Adequate Minimal	Yes No Somewhat	Lang. Arts Geography Soc. St./ History	Math Science Music/Art
	Abundant Adequate Minimal	Yes No Somewhat	Lang. Arts Geography Soc. St./ History	Math Science Music/Art

Sample Topic Breakout Sheet

Duplicate the Topic Breakout Sheet as many times as necessary so you are able to use one sheet for each of the main topic areas on your suggested topic list. To complete the sheet, write the main topic heading in the center top box. Next, write the subtopic headings in the top boxes on both sides of the main topic heading. Finally, write the common attributes in the column below the main topic heading.

Comanche	Sioux	Mohawk	Native American Tribes	Navaho	Chinook	Seminole
			original homeland / way of life / number of people			
			original dress, / utensils, weapons			
			language symbols / tribal government			
			treaties / historical battles			
			where tribe / lives today, / number of people			
			famous tribal / members from past / and present			

Sample Topic Breakout Sheet

Duplicate the Topic Breakout Sheet as many times as necessary so you are able to use one sheet for each of the main topic areas on your suggested topic list. To complete the sheet, write the main topic heading in the center top box. Next, write the subtopic headings in the top boxes on both sides of the main topic heading. Finally, write the common attributes in the column below the main topic heading.

Scott O'Dell	Lois Lowry	Avi	Newbery Award-Winning Authors	Jerry Spinelli	Katherine Paterson	Jean Craighead George
			early life— growing up			
			physical description and current family life			
			struggles— obstacles in life			
			accomplishments, other books besides Newbery			
			setting, themes, main characters of Newbery books			
			author's comments about his or her work—inspirations			

Sample Topic Breakout Sheet

Duplicate the Topic Breakout Sheet as many times as necessary so you are able to use one sheet for each of the main topic areas on your suggested topic list. To complete the sheet, write the main topic heading in the center top box. Next, write the subtopic headings in the top boxes on both sides of the main topic heading. Finally, write the common attributes in the column below the main topic heading.

Tree-Clinging Birds	Swallow-Like Birds	Duck-Like Birds	North American Birds	Owls	Hawk-Like Birds	Perching Birds
			description of male and female			
			habitat			
			description of voice or call			
			nesting			
			migration or range			
			personality, characteristics			

Topic Breakout Sheet

Step 2

Teacher decides how to form student groups based on selected criteria.

Forming student groups to maximize their chances for success takes critical as well as creative thinking. In *Expanding Cooperative Learning Through Group Investigation* (Teachers College Press, 1992), Sharan & Sharan acknowledge the challenges of group formation: "Since each classroom is a miniature society with its own unique composition, how to form small groups is a challenge teachers face anew every year." (p. 44)

Though group formation can be challenging, it is not impossible. Some suggestions for group formation follow.

Group Size

Two students is too few for a "group," but six students is too many. The best number of students for a research group is between three and five students. (Four students is perhaps the ideal number.) When it comes to group size, it's also important to remember that the larger the group, the more skilled students must be in communicating and sharing with others. In *Making Cooperative Learning Work* (Prentice Hall, 1998), Paul Vermette weighs in with his opinion about group size: "Few, if any, advantages accrue to teams larger than four at any grade level." (p. 73)

Criteria for Group Member Selection

If your student research groups will be together longer than a week and will be required to complete a complex research task such as the 10-step process described in this book, then teacher-selected groups are recommended. In *Learning Together and Alone* (Prentice Hall, 1987), Johnson & Johnson conclude that "often there is less on-task behavior in student-selected than in teacher-selected groups." (p. 49)

On the other hand, if your plans are to take a portion of the materials in this book to do a quick research group activity that will last a day or two, then random group membership is recommended. In *Cooperative Learning & Language Arts* (Kagan, 1994), Jeanne Stone describes the "Mix-Freeze-Group" selection strategy where students mix in the center of the room, the teacher calls out "freeze" and then counts out the students into groups. Another Stone idea is to decide group membership by the students' birthday month or favorite TV character. (You could use almost any criteria such as students who've read specific book titles or books written by specific authors.)

However, if a combination of teacher- and student-selected groups is what you desire, then there are ways of achieving this type of group membership as well. Two possible ways to gather student input for group member selection are to have students sign up to be in groups according to topic interest or have students write a list of names of other students with whom they would like to work. In both cases, you take the students' input under advisement, but you still determine the composition of each group.

Multiple Intelligences Criteria

If you decide to create the student groupings yourself, one recommended way is to assign students to groups based on the Theory of Multiple Intelligences (Gardner, 1983). Simply put, the Theory of Multiple Intelligences is based on the idea that although every person is a blending of all of the many intelligences, each of us has a stronger inclination toward the way we receive, store and process information. In other words, one or more "intelligences" dominate our learning style making us better at some things than others.

Since not only the various research student roles but also the group presentation roles require a variety of skills or, in other words, require the use of a variety of "intelligences," it seems reasonable to divide the student talent (and intelligences) among the groups. After all, each group could benefit from having an artist, writer, mathematician and consensus builder to name just a few of the skills from which to choose.

The eight intelligences are briefly described and a *general* description of students who may demonstrate each intelligence area is provided. Student descriptions come from information printed in Nancy Boyles' *The Learning Differences Sourcebook* (Lowell House, 1997).

A Student Group Planning Sheet based on the intelligences appears on page 21. One special

note: Using the Student Group Planning Sheet is in no way a scientific attempt to label students according to intelligences. It's merely a planning sheet to help facilitate group membership.

Verbal-Linguistic Intelligence

These students like to read, write and tell stories. They enjoy word games, jokes and puns. They also like to learn new words, speak in public and read poetry.

Logical-Mathematical Intelligence

These students like to work with numbers, analyze situations and use reasoning skills. They understand abstract patterns and like to have clear "right" or "wrong" answers.

Visual-Spatial Intelligence

These students like to look at maps, draw, paint and solve puzzles. They like to take things apart and put them back together and create three-dimensional objects.

Body-Kinesthetic Intelligence

These students like to play sports, use body language, do crafts and be physically active. They like to dance, act, mime and create mechanical projects.

Musical-Rhythmic Intelligence

These students like to listen to and play music. They enjoy singing, humming and creating tunes. They are aware of patterns in rhythm, pitch and timbre.

Interpersonal Intelligence

These students like to build consensus with others and enjoy working as team members. They like to lead, share and mediate as well as brainstorm ideas to get others' feedback.

Naturalist Intelligence

These students enjoy being outdoors, observing plants, collecting rocks and listening to the sounds in nature. They enjoy working with plants, animals and the environment.

Intrapersonal Intelligence

These students know their own strengths and weaknesses. They like to set their own learning goals. They learn by listening and observing others.

Room Arrangement

After working so hard to get just the right combination of students in each group, you don't want the groups to disintegrate into chaos because of poor room arrangement. Consider the following when arranging your room to maximize group success:

- Student group members should be "eye-to-eye and knee-to-knee" whether they're sitting on the floor, sitting around a table or sitting in a grouping of desks.

- Student groups should be separated so they do not disturb one another and you have a clear walking path to each group.

- Each student group should have a designated area where it always meets.

Group Member Information Exchange

One of the first things you may want your students to do once you have assigned them to a group is have them talk about any common free time they may have before, during or after school. Although much of the group research project will be completed during class time, there may be situations where members may have to exchange information, plan or even rehearse on their own time. Another suggestion is to have student members write the complete names and phone numbers of their group members on the inside of their paper project folder.

Student Group Planning Sheet

Name	Verbal	Math	Visual	Body	Music	Inter	Nature	Intra
1.								
2.								
3.								
4.								
5.								
6.								
7.								
8.								
9.								
10.								
11.								
12.								
13.								
14.								
15.								
16.								
17.								
18.								
19.								
20.								
21.								
22.								
23.								
24.								
25.								
26.								
27.								
28.								
29.								
30.								

	Group 1	Group 2	Group 3	Group 4	Group 5	Group 6
1.						
2.						
3.						
4.						
5.						

Step 3

Student groups engage in a planning session where they choose a topic, decide on Information Gathering Roles and specify deadlines.

Evaluation Explanation

Because Step 3 involves a number of different tasks, it may be better to complete some of the tasks in a morning session and the remainder in an afternoon session, or divide the tasks over a two-day period.

Regardless of how you divide Step 3, the first task is to explain to students how they will be evaluated. First, make overhead transparencies of the teacher and student evaluation sheets on pages 116 and 117. Describe how you plan to use the teacher evaluation sheet and identify which groups you will be evaluating during Step 3. If you plan to use the student evaluation sheet, briefly explain how to complete it by following the written directions.

What-Want-Where Chart

The next step in the planning session is for each group to select a research topic from the master list. Groups may want to review the Topic Breakout Sheets from Step 1 before choosing a topic. Once groups have chosen their topic, they may either use the completed Topic Breakout Sheet during the remainder of the Planning Session or revise the Topic Breakout Sheet to include different subtopics and/or attributes.

Once groups have their topic and their completed Topic Breakout Sheet, they should spend time discussing the topic and completing the What-Want-Where Chart that appears on page 24. This chart will help group members focus on what they know, what they want to know and where they think they can go to find their information.

Although groups should complete the What-Want-Where Chart together, each member should have his or her own copy to keep in his or her folder for future reference. In addition, it may be useful to make an overhead transparency of the chart and model or demonstrate how to complete the chart using a topic from the master list that wasn't chosen.

As you observe the groups, note any types of resources missing from their chart such as almanacs or atlases. These are the resources you will want to have your librarian or media specialist take extra time to explain to your students. (It's always a good idea to schedule a library resource review session with your school librarian so she or he can review where the school's research resources are and how to use them correctly. More specific suggestions for this review session appear in Step 4.) You may want to end part one of the planning session after each group has completed its chart.

Introduction of Information Gathering Roles

The second part of the planning session involves introducing students to the 11 Information Gathering Roles. Students should have a copy of each role sheet. Using an overhead transparency of each role, review each role's description that appears at the top of each sheet and answer questions. Because mini lessons explaining each role in detail are reserved for Step 4, it is not necessary to go into great detail about completing each role. Instead, students should have enough information in order to form an opinion about whether they would like to choose the role during this stage in the research process.

Planning Sheet

So far students have selected a topic and listed possible subtopics, discussed the topic, completed a What-Want-Where Chart and been introduced to the Information Gathering Roles. Now it's time to formulate their research plan and put it in writing by completing the Planning Sheet on page 25.

Each group completes its Planning Sheet and puts the sheet on the classroom bulletin board next to the display of the 10-step research process. Also on display on this bulletin board should be the classroom research project calendar. Each group's due date should be marked on the calendar. (You may want to give each group or student an individual calendar if you anticipate that getting work done on time will be a problem. You can duplicate the calendar on page 86 for this purpose.)

Troubleshooting Tip: Ways to Differ Topic Choices

If you do not want more than one group researching the same topic or you know there are not adequate research materials to accommodate two groups researching the same topic, you may want to do one of the following to avoid conflict:

1. Draw numbers for topics.

2. Have groups list their topic choices in order of preferences and try to accommodate their choices.

3. If some topics appear to be more popular than others, you may want to shorten the research project and give each group one subtopic to research instead of a complete topic. (You could then do three or four smaller research projects covering several different main topics instead of each group completing one large project.)

Troubleshooting Tip: Evaluation

Because of the two-part nature of Step 3, you will need to evaluate student groups during both the first and second parts of the planning session or else eliminate a portion of the assessment sheet. Also, only students who were in attendance for all of Step 3 should be asked to complete a Step 3 student evaluation.

What-Want-Where Chart

Directions: After discussing the topic as a group, complete the chart below.

Topic: _____   Date: _____

What we already know about the topic.	What we **want** to learn about the topic.	**Where** we think we might be able to find information about the topic.

Planning Sheet

Group Members

Today's Date: _____

1. _____
2. _____

3. _____
4. _____

5. _____

Goal Statement

We plan to research the main topic of _____ including the subtopics of

_____, _____, _____, _____,

_____ and _____.

We understand that as we gather information about our research topic, we may change subtopic categories by crossing out the old subtopic heading and writing in the new one.

Each group member has chosen an Information Gathering Role as listed below:

Role _____   Student _____

Role _____   Student _____

Role _____   Student _____

Role _____   Student _____

Role _____   Student _____

We agree to complete our Information Gathering Roles and meet for our group's Sharing Session by (write in date) _____.

We understand that while working on a research project, problems may arise. We also understand that while working as a group, problems may occur. We have listed some possible problems and solutions below.

Problem   **Solution**

_____   _____

_____   _____

_____   _____

Step 4

Students conduct research utilizing Information Gathering Roles.

At this point in the research project, students are very anxious to dig into their roles, but a quick review of library resources before allowing students to go off on their own could save a lot of time and frustration later. Also, providing students with five to 10-minute mini lessons on how to evaluate and document sources, how to complete a student self-evaluation, as well as how to do Boolean searches will keep them on the research track.

Mini Lesson: Locating and Using Research Resources

It's important to explain to your librarian or media specialist what your research project and process involve as well as providing him or her a list of topics students will be researching. Ask your librarian if he or she would provide each role group with a brief mini lesson describing how to use each resource material. Thus, all the Almanac Attackers from the groups would gather into a group, the Pamphlet Persons would gather into another group and so forth. Each mini lesson should include some of the following:

- the titles of the resources available in the school library and a quick review of the Dewey Decimal System
- where the resources are located
- how to access information in the resources
- when and where the resources may be used and if they can be checked out of the library
- interlibrary loan resources available

Mini Lesson: Evaluating Resources

You will want to provide mini lessons to different groups while the librarian is busy with groups of his or her own. You will especially want to work with any students who plan to conduct interviews. In addition, you will want to conduct mini lessons on notetaking strategies, how to evaluate resources, the importance of documenting sources of information and how to do a Boolean search. (If you do not know how to do a Boolean search on your library's computer system, have your media specialist teach you and write down the list of instructions so you can make copies for your students. Because each library's system is somewhat different, a step-by-step explanation cannot be provided here.)

Your mini lesson on how to evaluate resources should include four basic areas. Students should be taught to ask themselves the following four questions when choosing to use or not to use information from a resource:

- Is the information in the resource out of date?
- Is the information printed in a reliable newspaper, magazine, internet site or pamphlet?
- Is the information an opinion, or is the information based on factual research?
- Is the information one-sided with only one viewpoint presented?

It's important to point out to students that opinions are valuable sources of information as long as the opinion comes from an expert in the field being researched. In addition, information that is one-sided can also be valuable as long as the information is not distorted through omissions and is supported with factual research.

Mini Lesson: Documenting Resources and Completing Assessment Sheets

Another mini lesson you will want to present to your students is the importance of documenting where they get their research information. As students progress into the upper grades in school, they will be required to write research papers with specific research citation and bibliography requirements. Consequently, it's a good idea to get students used to the idea of citing their sources. (This also helps to discourage plagiarism.)

Each Information Gathering Role has a place to write down documentation information that is specific to that particular role. However, if you decide the documentation system on the role sheets is too complicated or if you want your students to remember a simple documenting system to use when doing general research, teach them the PPACT system. PPACT stands for:

P   Publisher
P   Page
A   Author
C   Copyright
T   Title

Utilizing this simple acronym will help students remember to document where they get their information regardless of the Information Gathering Role they choose.

As with previous evaluations, students should be aware of how they will be evaluated during this portion of the research process as well. Explain to the students how you plan to use the teacher evaluation sheet for Step 4. Since the information gathering stage occurs over a period of days, you may want to wait until students are almost done with their roles before you explain how they are to complete the student self-evaluation for Step 4.

Finally, after the mini lessons have been completed, students can begin on their own. However, it's important for students to remember that they are *gathering* information at this stage in the process. In order to gather information, students must first determine if the information they come across is useful or not. If they decide it is useful, they may want to photocopy some of the information, write down page numbers of resources to come back to or write brief summaries of the information. Students will process the research information for deeper understanding and organize it so it's useful at another stage in the process. So for now, students should be urged to gather as much useful information as they can about their topic.

Allow several class periods for students to complete their roles. (You may have to adjust due dates on the groups' Planning Sheets and class calendar depending upon how smoothly students take up their roles and begin gathering information for review later.) You will have to decide if you will allow students to change roles once the process has begun. In any case, duplicate several copies of each role sheet so students have easy access.

Step 5

Students take their completed role sheets to the group's planning session where they share information and available resources about the topic. Students select graphic organizers from the Information Processing and Organizing Roles.

Two-Part Session

It's natural for students to share in an informal way information with their group members during the information gathering stage of their research project. Since each student has decided to focus on one or two subtopics, if other group members find information about that subtopic during their own investigation, it's important for them to point out immediately the information to their group members, to jot down where they saw the information or make a copy of the information and take it to the group's sharing session.

Like the planning session in Step 3, Step 5 can be readily divided into two sessions and scheduled for a morning-afternoon session combination or scheduled over two days' class periods. Since the teacher and student evaluations relate only to the first part of Step 5, which is the group's sharing session, you should provide copies of the evaluation sheets to students and explain how you plan to evaluate each group and which groups are scheduled for evaluation. Also, briefly explain how students should complete the evaluation of their group's sharing session if you plan to use this evaluation.

Sharing Session Sheet

After you've briefly explained the teacher and student evaluations, groups should gather to begin their sharing session. Unlike informal sharing during the gathering stage, the sharing session is a more formal and systematic way of sharing information with other group members and involves completing the Sharing Session Sheet on page 30.

It's important to note that the sharing session not only allows group members the opportunity to share information resources, but it also gives the group the opportunity to refocus its research efforts if necessary by changing subtopics and attributes. If, during the gathering of information, a new subtopic or attribute emerges, group members can cross out subtopics and attributes and substitute new ones or add additional ones to their Planning Sheet. This addition and substitution allows the group's research efforts to influence the research project along with the group's preliminary plan.

Although the group should work together to complete the Sharing Session Sheet, each member should have his or her own sheet to complete and place in his or her project folder.

Introduction of Graphic Organizers

Now that students have gathered information, shared information resources and discussed their research subtopics, it's time for them to begin processing and organizing their research information for understanding so it can be used later in their group's research project presentation. Consequently, the second part of the sharing session involves introducing students to the eight Processing and Organizing Information Roles and the graphic organizers that accompany each set of roles.

Graphic organizers are visual thinking tools that help students process and understand relationships in research information; they also help improve students' memory of factual information (Black, 1990). Moreover, graphic organizers help students organize and keep track of large quantities of different types of information. Consequently, graphic organizers are especially useful for group research projects.

Modeling the Use of Graphic Organizers

You cannot assume that students know how to use graphic organizers, so it will be important for you to demonstrate how different organizers can be used to organize research information. Some suggestions appear below.

1. Based on the type of research topics your students are investigating, select five to 10 graphic organizers to model or select one or two organizers from each of the role areas. (For your convenience, a list of organizers and their suitability for use in different content areas appears on page 31.)

2. Explain to students that during this phase of their research project, they will have multiple roles and use a variety of organizers to help them process and organize the research information they've gathered.

3. Give each student copies of the organizers and make overhead transparencies.

4. Demonstrate how to complete the organizers using familiar or previously studied information. (Some examples appear on pages 91-95, but you are encouraged to complete each organizer using information your students already know. In this way, students will not focus on the research information but instead concentrate on how to use the organizer.)

5. Display copies of each of the organizers on a bulletin board or classroom wall. Tell students that if they wish to use any of the organizers that weren't demonstrated during the modeling session, they can see you for an explanation. (If several students wish to see how a particular organizer can be used, a better use of your time may be to continue with your whole-class modeling lesson.) However, it is not necessary nor desirable to model all 35 organizers at one time. As you continue doing research projects with your students, you will eventually introduce all 35 organizers to them.

6. Keep multiple copies of the graphic organizers you've introduced to students in an easily accessible place in the classroom.

7. Remind students that as they read through the research information they've gathered and as they continue to gather more information, they are to keep their completed graphic organizers in their project folders. They will need their completed graphic organizers for use in their group's preparing session, where they will decide how to combine their research information into one group presentation project.

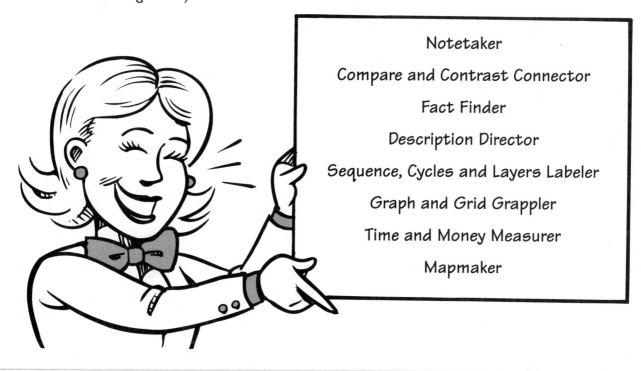

Notetaker

Compare and Contrast Connector

Fact Finder

Description Director

Sequence, Cycles and Layers Labeler

Graph and Grid Grappler

Time and Money Measurer

Mapmaker

Sharing Session Sheet

Group Members   Today's Date: _____

1. _____   2. _____

3. _____   4. _____

5. _____

Directions: Make a check mark in the space provided as your group completes the listed items below. Each group member should have his or her completed Information Gathering Role Sheet.

_____ Members should take out their completed Planning Sheet and What-Want-Where Chart from their project folders.

_____ Members should tell what subtopic(s) they're researching and describe the information they've gathered and from what sources.

_____ Members should exchange any information or resource titles about other members' subtopics.

_____ Members should review Planning Sheet and cross out and write in any new subtopics or attributes that might have emerged as a result of the group's research.

_____ Members should review their What-Want-Where Chart and make suggestions about where to find information to other group members who may be having difficulty finding information.

_____ Members must correct any information on their Planning Sheet that is displayed in the classroom.

_____ Members must agree on the date they will meet for their preparing session where they will decide how they will combine their research information into one group project presentation.

_____ Members must have the date for their preparing session approved by the teacher and recorded on the classroom research project calendar.

Information and suggestions my group members gave to me: _____

_____

_____

_____

_____

_____

30

Step 6

Students process and organize information using graphic organizers.

Once students have gathered research information, they need to process it and organize it in order for the information to be useful. Only after the information is meaningful to students can it then be used to create a group project presentation.

The Processing and Organizing Information Roles include 35 different graphic organizers divided into eight categories that have been labeled as student roles. Students should be encouraged to use as many different organizers as they need regardless of the number of roles involved.

By using the various roles and accompanying graphic organizers, students will be able to decide which information they wish to include in their research, and then process and organize the information so that it's meaningful and useful.

The roles and accompanying graphic organizers are listed here. Although each graphic organizer is extremely versatile, for your convenience, they have been labeled as to their suitability for use with different content area research projects.

Many of the organizers are suitable for all subject areas and are labeled *ALL*. The remaining content areas are labeled as follows:

LA: Language Arts
SH: Social Studies and/or History
MA: Music and/or Art
G: Geography
M: Math
S: Science

Notetaker

Traditional (ALL)
Web (ALL)

Compare and Contrast Connector

Venn (ALL)
Pyramid (ALL)

Fact Finder

Fact Card (ALL)
Multiple Facts: List (ALL)
Multiple Facts: Boxes (ALL)
Multiple Facts: Categories (ALL)
The Lazy L (ALL)
Event Description (LA/SH/MA/G/S)

Description Director

Person Portrait (LA/MA/SH)
Place Pyramid (LA/SH/G)
Web Box (ALL)
Illustration Illuminator (MA/G/S/SH)

Sequence, Cycles and Layers Labeler

Cycle (SH/G/S)
Sequence (SH/MA/G/S)
Layer (G/S)
Cylinder (SH/G/S)
For and Against (ALL)
Cause and Effect (ALL)
Beginning-Middle-Ending (ALL)

Graph and Grid Grappler

Large Graph (G/M/S/SH)
Small Graph (G/M/S/SH)
Dots (G/M/S)

Time and Money Measurer

Clock Constructor (SH/G/S)
Calendar Counter (ALL)
Time Liner (ALL)
Currency Converter (G/LA/SH/MA)

Mapmaker

United States (G/SH/MA/S)
World (G/SH/MA/S)
Mexico (G/SH/MA/S)
Canada (G/SH/MA/S)

Teacher and student evaluations are available to assess this portion of the research process and should be briefly explained prior to the students beginning Step 6.

Step 7

Student groups meet in a preparing session where they discuss their research information, assess group talents, choose a group presentation role, divide up responsibilities and specify a presentation date.

At this point in the research process, each student should have his or her chosen subtopic(s) and attributes completely researched and information recorded on graphic organizers. During the group's preparing session, members should discuss the research information they've gathered and decide how to integrate the information into a group presentation. However, before groups can meet to share information and decide the type of presentation they'd like to do, you must review the teacher and student evaluations that are available to assess Steps 7 and 8. (The first part of the evaluation assesses the group's preparing session while the second part of the evaluation assesses the group's preparations for its group project presentation.)

Introduction of Presentation Roles

Although you've explained how the groups will be evaluated in their preparing session, it's not yet time for student groups to gather. Instead, you should introduce the eight Information Presenting Roles to the entire class.

First, give each student copies of the eight roles and make overhead transparencies to use during your presentation. Introduce each of the eight roles, and ask students for suggestions as to how each could be used with their research topic and information. (The roles are extremely versatile and can be used with topics that are geography-oriented, science-oriented, history-oriented, music- and art-oriented and language arts-oriented.)

In addition to an explanation and discussion of the roles, you may want to model one or two of the presentation roles for your class. To do this, select a topic which is familiar to your students and demonstrate how to create a culture kit or postcard display by following the role sheet's directions. The last part of your modeling session should be an actual oral presentation.

A final component in your introduction of the presentation roles is to give students a copy of the teacher evaluation rubric that you will use to assess each group's presentation. Explain how you intend to use this form to give each group a grade on their presentation. Stress the qualities that make presentations rated "excellent" and "good."

Preparing Sheet

Students are ready to gather into groups and complete their Preparing Sheet. Completing the Preparing Sheet may take well over an hour or perhaps longer if the groups are larger than four. Set a realistic time deadline so students have enough time to thoroughly discuss what they need to, but don't get bogged down with preparation details.

Students should keep their completed Preparing Sheet in their project folder. However, as with the Planning Sheet from Step 3, each group should complete an extra Preparing Sheet and put it on the bulletin board next to the classroom calendar. Each group's presentation date should also be recorded on the classroom calendar.

Special Note: Encourage groups to consider a variety of presentation roles; however, if every group in your class chooses the same presentation role, it won't matter if they've chosen different research topics.

Preparing Sheet

Group Members   Today's Date: _____

1. _____   2. _____

3. _____   4. _____

5. _____

Directions: Your group has selected a main topic and each of you has gathered research information about your subtopic(s) and recorded the information onto graphic organizers. Now it is time to combine the information you've gathered to create a group presentation project. Before you decide your group's Information Presentation Role, think about and discuss the questions below:

- What are some special talents your group members have? (Acting, drawing, public speaking, playing a musical instrument, cooking, computer skills, languages, videotaping, organizing, planning, paying attention to details, building things, growing things, etc.)

- How can you use the different research information you've gathered to create a group project? (Members should have their completed graphic organizers with them.)

Next, make a list on the back of this paper of two or three possible presentation projects. Write the positives and negatives of each project. Finally, complete the remainder of this sheet.

The Information Presentation Role we've chosen is _____.

We've divided the project and responsibilities among group members as follows:

Name	Project Part	Student's Responsibilities
_____	_____	_____
_____	_____	_____
_____	_____	_____
_____	_____	_____
_____	_____	_____

The materials that we will need to complete this project include _____
_____.

The most difficult part of this project will be _____
_____.

We will be ready to present our project to the entire class on _____.

Step 8

Groups complete the preparations for their presentations.

Groups will need their own special place not only to prepare and rehearse their presentations but also to keep their materials and completed work. It's best to assign group space after each group has declared its presentation project since some groups may need floor space while other groups may need desk space or access to the computer lab. Paper bags or plastic tubs with group members' names work well for materials and completed work.

Groups will need several hours over the course of several days to complete their projects if they are expected to do all or most of the work in class. To keep the groups focused and making progress, complete a section of the Daily Group Progress Log each day for each group. Display the logs next to each group's Preparing Sheet. (The Daily Group Progress Log appears on page 35.) Recording this information will keep you informed of each group's progress and will allow each group to see its progress as well.

Step 9

Groups complete their presentations for the entire class.

Groups present their projects to the class on their designated dates or times. You may wish to videotape the presentations and watch the taped presentations at a "wrap party" at the end of the research project. Another suggestion is to invite students from the lower grades to watch.

A teacher assessment rubric is available for evaluating group projects.

Step 10

Students complete a final assessment of the entire research project experience.

Doing a final student assessment of the research project experience will help you make plans for the next research project by discovering what worked and what didn't work for your students. The assessment should be done as soon as possible after the project experience has been completed but *not* during a "wrap party."

The assessment will give you a general overview of how the students responded to the project as well as some specifics about various steps in the research process. Along with your own notes and observations, you'll be able to begin planning your next research project–from start to finish!

Daily Group Progress Log

Group Members

1. _____   2. _____

3. _____   4. _____

5. _____

Today's Date: _____   Our group plans to work on this specific part or parts of

the project: _____.

Tomorrow we plan to work on the following: _____

_____

- -

Today's Date: _____   Our group plans to work on this specific part or parts of

the project: _____.

Tomorrow we plan to work on the following: _____

_____

- -

Today's Date: _____   Our group plans to work on this specific part or parts of

the project: _____.

Tomorrow we plan to work on the following: _____

_____

- -

Today's Date: _____   Our group plans to work on this specific part or parts of

the project: _____.

Tomorrow we plan to work on the following: _____

_____

Information Gathering Roles

In group investigation, students act as creative research scholars, producing their own knowledge.

Elizabeth Cohen
Designing Groupwork

Internet Investigator

Encyclopedia Explorer

Almanac Attacker

Dictionary Detective

In-Depth Interviewer

Multimedia Messenger

Periodical Person

Newspaper Notetaker

Atlas Analyzer

Pamphlet Person

Book Browser

Name _____

Internet Investigator

Your role as your group's Internet Investigator is to jump onto the World Wide Web information highway and find reliable and relevant information about your research topic. Because by some estimates the web is doubling every month with well over 85,000 new sites being added each month (Miller xvii), it's important you know where to look for information.

Browsing through web sites can be a lot of fun if you have free time, but when it comes to doing research, it's better to have specific addresses. This is where web directories can help you. Like categorized telephone books, web directories can tell you specific addresses you can use to connect you directly to valuable sites. (Some helpful addresses appear on page 38.)

Your teacher, librarian or media specialist will help you locate and use web directories. Your role as Internet Investigator is to search out different sites and decide whether the site would be useful to investigate in more detail at a later time.

As you conduct your initial web search, complete the form below and bring this sheet to your group's sharing session.

Topic: _____ Web Address: _____

Access Date: _____ Specific Features: _____

Comments About Information at This Site: _____

_____

- -

Topic: _____ Web Address: _____

Access Date: _____ Specific Features: _____

Comments About Information at This Site: _____

_____

- -

Topic: _____ Web Address: _____

Access Date: _____ Specific Features: _____

Comments About Information at This Site: _____

_____

Name _____

Internet Investigator

Using a web dictionary such as *The Internet Resource Directory* (Libraries Unlimited, 1998) can help you quickly locate valuable web sites such as the ones below.

Kids Web: **http://www.npac.syr.edu/textbook/kidsweb/**

The Virtual Schoolhouse: **http://sunsite.unc.edu/cisco/schoolhouse.html**

Internet Public Library: **http://ipl.sils.umich.edu/**

World Wide Web Virtual Library History Resources: **http://history.cc.ukans.edu/history/WWW_history_main.html**

The Library of Congress: **http://www.loc.gov**

The 50 States of the United States: **http://www.scvol.com/States/fileindx.html**

Smithsonian Institution's Natural History Web: **http://nmnhwww.si.edu/nmnhweb.html**

The Metropolitan Museum of Art, New York City: **http://www.metmuseum.org**

Topic: _____ Web Address: _____

Access Date: _____ Specific Features: _____

Comments About Information at This Site: _____

_____

– –

Topic: _____ Web Address: _____

Access Date: _____ Specific Features: _____

Comments About Information at This Site: _____

_____

– –

Topic: _____ Web Address: _____

Access Date: _____ Specific Features: _____

Comments About Information at This Site: _____

_____

– –

Topic: _____ Web Address: _____

Access Date: _____ Specific Features: _____

Comments About Information at This Site: _____

_____

Name _____

ENCYCLOPEDIA EXPLORER

Your role as the Encyclopedia Explorer is to gather research information from several encyclopedias. Encyclopedias are great places to begin your research or to add to your research because they provide a broad overview of your topic. General encyclopedias are usually in alphabetical sets and contain information on a variety of subjects. Special encyclopedias have information on specific subjects. For example, the *Encyclopedia of the Cold War* (Facts on File, 1994) and *The Baseball Encyclopedia* (Macmillan, 1996) are examples of special encyclopedias. Check to see if special encyclopedias are available on your topic.

In addition to book sets of encyclopedias, excellent CD-ROM encyclopedias such as Microsoft's *Encarta*, Grolier's and Compton's are available and can make finding research information interesting and fun. Finally, you can go online and explore encyclopedias such as *Encyclopedia Smithsonian* at **http://www.si.edu/resource/faq/start.htm**.

Keep track of the encyclopedias you explore by completing the information below. Take this information to your group's sharing session.

General Encyclopedia

Name of Encyclopedia: _____

Subject Heading or Article Title: _____

Author: _____ Volume: _____ Page(s): _____ Copyright: _____

Special Encyclopedia

Name of Encyclopedia: _____

Subject Heading or Article Title: _____

Author: _____ Volume: _____ Page(s): _____ Copyright: _____

CD-ROM Encyclopedia

Name of Encyclopedia: _____

Subject Heading or Article Title: _____

Author: _____ Edition: _____ Copyright: _____

Online Encyclopedia

Name of Encyclopedia: _____

Online Address: _____

Subject Heading or Article Title: _____

Author: _____ Date You Got Information: _____

ALMANAC ATTACKER

Your role as the Almanac Attacker is to find factual information about your research topic from a variety of almanacs. Because most almanacs are published every year, the information about sports, people and governments is current. Some almanacs focus on one specific topic such as weather or science. However, almost all almanacs contain useful charts, tables and calendars.

Of course online information is available. You can search the CIA World Factbook for facts about countries around the world at **http://www.odci.gov/cia/publications/factbook/index.html**. You can also check out different time zones in cities across the United States and the rest of the world at The Directorate of Time, U.S. Naval Observatory's site at **http://www.tycho.usno.navy.mil** and have fun converting the world's various money at The OANDA Currency Converter site at **http://www.oanda.com/cgi-bin-ncc**.

To keep track of the current facts related to your research topic, complete the chart below and take this sheet to your group's sharing session.

Title of Almanac: _____

Online Address: _____ or Publisher: _____

Date You Got Information: _____ or Copyright: _____

Topic: _____

Fact: _____ Fact: _____

Fact: _____ Fact: _____

- -

Topic: _____

Fact: _____ Fact: _____

Fact: _____ Fact: _____

- -

Topic: _____

Fact: _____ Fact: _____

Fact: _____ Fact: _____

- -

Topic: _____

Fact: _____ Fact: _____

Fact: _____ Fact: _____

Name _____

ALMANAC ATTACKER

To keep track of the current facts related to your research topic, complete the chart below and take this sheet to your group's sharing session.

Title of Almanac: _____

Online Address: _____ or Publisher: _____

Date You Got Information: _____ or Copyright: _____

Topic: _____

Fact: _____ Fact: _____

Fact: _____ Fact: _____

- -

Topic: _____

Fact: _____ Fact: _____

Fact: _____ Fact: _____

- -

Topic: _____

Fact: _____ Fact: _____

Fact: _____ Fact: _____

- -

Topic: _____

Fact: _____ Fact: _____

Fact: _____ Fact: _____

- -

Topic: _____

Fact: _____ Fact: _____

Fact: _____ Fact: _____

- -

Topic: _____

Fact: _____ Fact: _____

Fact: _____ Fact: _____

DICTIONARY DETECTIVE

Your role as the Dictionary Detective is to locate valuable research information in different dictionaries. While an encyclopedia can give you a brief overview of your research topic, a dictionary can provide you with specific information about unfamiliar words in an easy-to-use alphabetical listing. Most importantly, however, special dictionaries can provide you with information that may be difficult to find in other reference materials. For example, *The Dictionary of Imaginary Places* (Harcourt Brace, 1987) is an alphabetical listing of such places as Shangri-La and Oz that are mentioned in literature. Many other special dictionaries focus on specific topics such as biographies, cultures and art.

Helpful dictionaries are also available online. Carnegie Mellon University's site at **http://www.cs.cmu.edu/Web/references.html** also includes French, German and Japanese dictionaries. If you come across unfamiliar acronyms or abbreviations in your research, go to **http://www.ucc.ie/infor/net/acronyms/index.html**. For an overall easy-to-use dictionary, *Webster's Dictionary and Thesaurus Searchable* can be reached at **http://www.m-w.com/netdict.htm**.

Record your information on the form below and take this information to your group's sharing session.

Title of Dictionary: _____

Online Address: _____ or Publisher: _____

Date You Got Information: _____ or Copyright: _____

Word	**Definition • Translation • Illustration**
_____	_____
_____	_____
_____	_____
_____	_____
_____	_____

Name _____

DICTIONARY DETECTIVE

Record your information from your dictionary sources and take this information to your group's sharing session.

Title of Dictionary: _____

Online Address: _____ or Publisher: _____

Date You Got Information: _____ or Copyright: _____

Word | **Definition • Translation • Illustration**

_____   _____

_____   _____

_____   _____

```
[empty box]
```

Title of Dictionary: _____

Online Address: _____ or Publisher: _____

Date You Got Information: _____ or Copyright: _____

Word | **Definition • Translation • Illustration**

_____   _____

_____   _____

_____   _____

```
[empty box]
```

In-Depth Interviewer

Your role as an In-Depth Interviewer is to interview someone who is an expert in the area of your research topic or who has firsthand knowledge about your topic. A person is said to have firsthand knowledge if he or she actually witnessed an event at the time it happened.

In order for your interview to be successful, you must plan ahead. Use the checklist below and the Interview Planning Sheet to help you prepare for your interview.

Sometimes conducting an interview face-to-face is not possible because the person you want to interview lives too far away. If distance is a problem, you may want to conduct your interview by an e-mail chat online. If you do so, you must have approval from your teacher. Another way to interview is to fax a set of questions to the person you want to interview and have him or her fax the answers back to you. If you conduct an interview using the fax machine, make sure you follow up with a telephone call to make sure you understand all the information and ask follow-up questions. As with the e-mail chat, you must have your teacher's approval to conduct an interview using the fax machine and the telephone.

Interview Checklist

Before Your Interview

_____ Read about your topic so you have a basic understanding of it. As you read, write possible questions.

_____ Ask your group members for questions they would like you to ask in the interview.

_____ Read through all of your questions and choose the best ones to ask first. Make sure your questions don't require just a "yes" or "no" answer. Instead, say, "Tell me about the time . . ." or "Describe what you saw."

_____ Confirm the date, time and location of your interview with the person you're interviewing. Remind the person of your topic and type of research project. Ask permission to take a tape recorder if you plan to use one.

_____ Practice asking your questions and jotting down quick notes as a response. If you plan to use a tape recorder, practice using it and changing batteries and tapes.

During Your Interview

_____ Ask your most important question first then LISTEN to the answers.

_____ If you don't understand an answer, ask for an explanation.

_____ Look at the person you're interviewing.

_____ Wait until the person you're interviewing has finished his or her answer before asking another question.

_____ Take brief notes during the interview. At the end of the interview, quickly look over your notes and ask any final questions.

After Your Interview

_____ Immediately after your interview, listen to your tape recording and write out your notes so you don't forget the information you've gathered.

_____ Send the person you interviewed a thank-you note.

Name _____

In-Depth Interviewer

Complete the planning sheet below before you interview. Use the sheet during the interview to write quick notes about answers to your questions. After your interview, listen to the tape recording of your interview (if you have one) and write in detail the notes you've written. Take this planning sheet and your completed notes to your group's sharing session.

Interview Planning Sheet

The interview will take place on (date) _____ at (time) _____

at (location) _____ .

The person I am interviewing is _____ .

The reason this person is a good person to interview about my topic is because _____

_____ .

Topic Areas	**Questions-Answers**
	Q: _____
	A: _____
	_____
	Q: _____
	A: _____
	_____
	Q: _____
	A: _____
	_____
	Q: _____
	A: _____
	_____

MULTIMEDIA MESSENGER

Your role as the Multimedia Messenger is to locate any video-tapes, audiotapes, computer programs or software such as CD-ROMs and videodiscs, as well as any compact discs, television programs or films that can provide valuable information about your research topic.

Often public as well as school libraries have special multimedia collections on everything including countries, famous people, historical events and music. Although as the Multimedia Messenger you have several resources to check, finding what you're looking for won't be too difficult because all multimedia resources are listed in the library's card or electronic catalog.

As you search through various multimedia, record the information below and take this sheet to your group's sharing session. (Note: You can check out the Multimedia Library on the World Wide Web at **http://kinga.cyf-kr.edu.pl/mmedia/** but a word of caution: you often need special computer software to download sound and videos so you can hear and see them. Consequently, you should get your teacher's approval before downloading anything.)

Videocassette   **Description of Contents**

Title: _____   _____

Distributed by: _____   _____

Copyright: _____ Length: _____   _____

Audiocassette or Compact Disc   **Description of Contents**

Title: _____   _____

Distributed by: _____   _____

Copyright: _____ Length: _____   _____

Television Program   **Description of Contents**

Title of Program/Episode/Segment: _____   _____

Title of TV Show: _____   _____

Station: _____ Air Date: _____ _____

Film   **Description of Contents**

Title: _____   _____

Director: _____   _____

Distributed by: _____   _____

Copyright: _____

Name _____

MULTIMEDIA MESSENGER

As you search through various multimedia, record the information below and take this sheet with you to your group's sharing session.

CD-ROM or Videodisc

Title: _____

Distributed by: _____

Edition: _____ Copyright: _____

Videocassette

Title: _____

Distributed by: _____

Copyright: _____ Length: _____

CD-ROM or Videodisc

Title: _____

Distributed by: _____

Edition: _____ Copyright: _____

Description of Contents

_____

_____

_____

Description of Contents

_____

_____

_____

Description of Contents

_____

_____

_____

Additional Multimedia

Format: Videocassette   Audiocassette   Compact Disc   Television   Film   CD-ROM   Videodisc

Description of Contents and Identifying Information: _____

_____

_____

Format: Videocassette   Audiocassette   Compact Disc   Television   Film   CD-ROM   Videodisc

Description of Contents and Identifying Information: _____

_____

_____

PERIODICAL PERSON

Hundreds of magazines are published weekly, monthly or quarterly on topics ranging from mountain climbing to money. Your role as Periodical Person is to search different magazines and find information that is related to your specific research topic.

Your school library may have the *Reader's Guide to Periodical Literature*. This is an index of magazines that lists articles by subject and author. Your school library may also have CD-ROM indexes such as *TOM (Text on Microfilm)*, *SIRS (Social Issues Resource Service)*, *Wilsondisc* or *Infotrac*. Using CD-ROM indexes can be convenient but somewhat tricky. Ask your teacher, librarian or media specialist how to do a Boolean search. A Boolean search will help you narrow your topic and provide you with full text and/or summaries of articles that are directly related to your topic. (Note: These indexes may also contain newspaper articles.)

In addition to the *Reader's Guide* and CD-ROM indexes, you can search magazines online. *Smithsonian Magazine* is at **http://www.smithsonianmag.si.edu**, *Time Daily* is at **http://pathfinder.com/time/daily** while *Time for Kids* is at **http://www.pathfinder.com/TFK**. One additional news magazine, *U.S. News & World Report Online,* is at **http://www.usnews.com**.

As you look for information in various magazines that is directly related to your topic, record your information below and bring this sheet to your group's sharing session.

Title of Article: _____ Author: _____

Name of Magazine: _____ Article Page(s): _____ Vol.: _____

Online Address: _____ or CD-ROM Index: _____

Date You Got Information: _____ or Publication Date: _____

Summary of Article as It Relates to Your Topic: _____

_____

_____

- -

Title of Article: _____ Author: _____

Name of Magazine: _____ Article Page(s): _____ Vol.: _____

Online Address: _____ or CD-ROM Index: _____

Date You Got Information: _____ or Publication Date: _____

Summary of Article as It Relates to Your Topic: _____

_____

_____

Name _____

PERIODICAL PERSON

Your role as Periodical Person is to search different magazines and find information that is related to your specific research topic. As you look for information, complete the form below and take this sheet to your group's sharing session.

Title of Article: _____ Author: _____

Name of Magazine: _____ Article Page(s): _____ Vol.: _____

Online Address: _____ or CD-ROM Index: _____

Date You Got Information: _____ or Publication Date: _____

Summary of Article as It Relates to Your Topic: _____

_____

_____

- -

Title of Article: _____ Author: _____

Name of Magazine: _____ Article Page(s): _____ Vol.: _____

Online Address: _____ or CD-ROM Index: _____

Date You Got Information: _____ or Publication Date: _____

Summary of Article as It Relates to Your Topic: _____

_____

_____

- -

TTitle of Article: _____ Author: _____

Name of Magazine: _____ Article Page(s): _____ Vol.: _____

Online Address: _____ or CD-ROM Index: _____

Date You Got Information: _____ or Publication Date: _____

Summary of Article as It Relates to Your Topic: _____

_____

_____

NEWSPAPER NOTETAKER

Newspapers provide up-to-the-minute information such as facts, statistics and quotations. Often photographs, maps, charts and graphs are included with stories. In addition, newspapers follow current events as they happen and update stories from day to day, thus making newspapers valuable sources of research information.

Your role as Newspaper Notetaker is to find information about your research topic in different newspapers. In addition to browsing through stacks of newspapers, you may want to use a newspaper index and look at newspapers on microfilm. Some valuable indexes include *Facts on File, Editorials on File* and *National Newspaper Index*. Also, many newspapers are online and can be reached simply by typing in their names after the **http://www**. Some that you might want to look at include *The New York Times* at **http://www.nytimes.com**, *USA Today* at **http://www.usatoday.com** and *The Washington Post* at **http://www.washingtonpost.com**.

Record your information on the form below and bring this information to your group's sharing session.

Newspaper's Name: _____   Publication Date: _____

Title of Article: _____

Byline (Reporter or News Service): _____

Page(s): _____   Newspaper Section or Web Address: _____

Summary of Information: _____

_____

_____

- -

Newspaper's Name: _____   Publication Date: _____

Title of Article: _____

Byline (Reporter or News Service): _____

Page(s): _____   Newspaper Section or Web Address: _____

Summary of Information: _____

_____

_____

Name _____

Newspaper Notetaker

Newspaper's Name: _____ Publication Date: _____

Title of Article: _____

Byline (Reporter or News Service): _____

Page(s): _____ Newspaper Section or Web Address: _____

Summary of Information: _____

_____

_____

- -

Newspaper's Name: _____ Publication Date: _____

Title of Article: _____

Byline (Reporter or News Service): _____

Page(s): _____ Newspaper Section or Web Address: _____

Summary of Information: _____

_____

_____

- -

Newspaper's Name: _____ Publication Date: _____

Title of Article: _____

Byline (Reporter or News Service): _____

Page(s): _____ Newspaper Section or Web Address: _____

Summary of Information: _____

_____

_____

ATLAS ANALYZER

Your role as Atlas Analyzer is to gather research information from a variety of atlases. An atlas can help you discover everything from the location of a national park to the number of county seats in a state. More than just a collection of maps, atlases include detailed descriptions as well as charts and tables that illustrate a particular subject.

In addition to providing information about products, climate and resources, many specialized atlases exist. For example, some specialized atlases include the *Atlas of Rain Forests* (Raintree, 1997), the *Atlas of Endangered Animals* (Facts on File, 1993) and *The West Point Atlas of American Wars* (Henry Holt, 1995).

Also, excellent atlas resources exist online. You can click onto an interactive globe at Xerox's PARC Map Viewer site at **http://pubweb.parc.xerox.com/map** or look at Earth from outer space at Earth's Viewer's site at **http://fourmilab.ch/earthview/vplanet.html**. In addition, you can get the World Atlas at **http://cliffie.nosc.mil/~NATLAS/atlas/index.html** as well as Flags of the world at **http://flags.cesi.it/flags**. Finally, if you're looking for up-to-the-minute weather information, go to the WeatherNet site at **http://cirrus.sprl.umich.edu/wxnet/wxnetplus.html**.

Because atlases provide a great deal of information, you will have to decide what information you wish to use for your research project. Use the atlas's table of contents and/or index to help you locate your research area of information. As you read through the atlas, write the page number and a brief description of the useful information. Record this information below and bring this sheet to your group's sharing session.

Title of Atlas: _____

Online Address: _____ Date You Got Information: _____

or

Author: _____ Publisher: _____ Copyright: _____

Page	**Description of Useful Information**
_____	_____
_____	_____
_____	_____
_____	_____
_____	_____
_____	_____

Name _____

ATLAS ANALYZER

As you read through the atlas, write the page number and a brief description of the useful information. Record this information below and take this sheet to your group's sharing session.

Title of Atlas: _____

Online Address: _____

Date You Got Information: _____

or

Author: _____ Publisher: _____ Copyright: _____

Page	Description of Useful Information
_____	_____
_____	_____
_____	_____
_____	_____
_____	_____

- -

Title of Atlas: _____

Online Address: _____ Date You Got Information: _____

or

Author: _____ Publisher: _____ Copyright: _____

Page	Description of Useful Information
_____	_____
_____	_____
_____	_____
_____	_____

PAMPHLET PERSON

Often libraries will have what is called a vertical file, information file or pamphlet file collection. This research information is most often in the form of booklets, brochures and leaflets published by companies, organizations, schools and government agencies. (If you've ever stopped at a state travel information center or visited an agency like the Red Cross, you would recognize the types of booklets and brochures contained in a library's pamphlet file.)

As the Pamphlet Person, it is your role to find different pamphlets and brochures related to your research topic. In addition to going through your library's pamphlet file, one of the best ways to get pamphlets and brochures is to ask for them either by writing a letter, e-mailing your request or requesting information online. (Online requests must be approved by your teacher.)

You can look in reference books for mailing addresses of companies, organizations and schools as well as for the addresses of specific people. Finding e-mail addresses may be a bit more difficult. However, you can often get e-mail addresses by visiting specific web pages. For example, you can get e-mail addresses of congressional members at **http://congress.org** and senators at **http://www.senate.gov**. Most web pages of schools, organizations and state governments will tell you how to get more information in the form of brochures and pamphlets by providing you with either a mailing address, telephone number or e-mail address.

To keep track of the information you request and receive, complete the form below and take this sheet to your group's sharing session.

Request-Receipt Record

Topic: _____

Organization/Person: _____

Address (e-mail/www/mailing): _____

Date Request Was Made: _____ Date Material Received: _____

No Response: _____

- -

Request-Receipt Record

Topic: _____

Organization/Person: _____

Address (e-mail/www/mailing): _____

Date Request Was Made: _____ Date Material Received: _____

No Response: _____

Name _____

PAMPHLET PERSON

To keep track of the information you review, complete the form below and take this sheet to your group's sharing session.

Type of Material: Pamphlet   Booklet   Brochure   Other _____

Title: _____ Author (if known): _____

Publisher or Distributed by: _____

Number of Pages: _____ Publication Date (if known): _____

The following supporting facts directly relate to the research topic of: _____

1. _____   2. _____

3. _____   4. _____

- -

Type of Material: Pamphlet   Booklet   Brochure   Other _____

Title: _____ Author (if known): _____

Publisher or Distributed by: _____

Number of Pages: _____ Publication Date (if known): _____

The following supporting facts directly relate to the research topic of: _____

1. _____   2. _____

3. _____   4. _____

- -

Type of Material: Pamphlet   Booklet   Brochure   Other _____

Title: _____ Author (if known): _____

Publisher or Distributed by: _____

Number of Pages: _____ Publication Date (if known): _____

The following supporting facts directly relate to the research topic of: _____

1. _____   2. _____

3. _____   4. _____

BOOK BROWSER

Your role as the Book Browser is to find books that contain valuable information about your research topic. This may sound like an easy task–and it is–if you know what you're looking for and where to look for it.

First, you may want to search not only your school library for books but also to search your public library as well. Also, you may want to consider asking for a book or books through your library's interlibrary loan services. Getting the book may take a few days, but if it's a book that's just right for your research project, it's worth the wait. (If you plan to use interlibrary loan books, make your requests early in your search process.)

The types of books you're looking for include nonfiction, biographies and autobiographies, specific reference books, and in some instances, fiction books. When looking through the reference book collection, remember that your other group members will be looking at encyclopedias, dictionaries, almanacs and atlases; however, there are many other specific reference books focusing on one specific topic. These are the types of reference books you're looking for.

When looking through your library's nonfiction book collection, use the card or computerized card catalog. Use several different topic headings to help you locate the area or areas that contain information about your topic. (Note: Although you are looking for books that focus on your topic, be aware that other books may have a chapter or two about your topic. For example, if your research topic is child labor, you may also want to look in books about the rise of unions because they helped enact child labor laws.) Once you find the general area and perhaps have the titles of a few specific books, go to that area of books and **browse** through the entire section of books! Look at all the books that may have something about your topic. Examine each book's table of contents and its index. Choose the books that are the most current and have the most information about your specific research topic area.

Biographies and autobiographies can be valuable resources not only about people but historical events as well. Often biographies and autobiographies contain primary source information such as photographs, letters and documents. Based on the Dewey Decimal System, biographies and autobiographies can be found in the 920s. (Once again, don't forget to check each book's table of contents and index.)

One final area for research is the fiction book collection, which is arranged alphabetically according to the author's last name. For example, if you are researching a specific time period, country or famous person, you may want to read books written during that time, in that country or by the famous person. Reading fiction books related to your nonfiction research topic will help you better understand the facts, statistics and details you collect.

It's important that you keep track of the books you plan to use for research. In order to do this, complete the information below and on the next page and take both sheets to your group's sharing session.

This book will be most valuable for research in the topic area of _____

because it contains: _____

Call Number: _____   Library or Loan: School   Public   Interlibrary

Title: _____   Author: _____

Publisher: _____   Publication Place: _____   Copyright: _____

Name _____

BOOK BROWSER

Complete the following information as you browse through the various book collections. Take this completed sheet to your group's sharing session.

This book will be most valuable for research in the topic area of _____

because it contains _____.

Call Number: _____ Library or Loan: School   Public   Interlibrary

Title: _____ Author: _____

Publisher: _____ Publication Place: _____ Copyright: _____

- -

This book will be most valuable for research in the topic area of _____

because it contains _____.

Call Number: _____ Library or Loan: School   Public   Interlibrary

Title: _____ Author: _____

Publisher: _____ Publication Place: _____ Copyright: _____

- -

This book will be most valuable for research in the topic area of _____.

because it contains _____

Call Number: _____ Library or Loan: School   Public   Interlibrary

Title: _____ Author: _____

Publisher: _____ Publication Place: _____ Copyright: _____

- -

This book will be most valuable for research in the topic area of _____

because it contains _____.

Call Number: _____ Library or Loan: School   Public   Interlibrary

Title: _____ Author: _____

Publisher: _____ Publication Place: _____ Copyright: _____

Information Processing and Organizing Roles

*Graphic organizers are "diagrammatic outlines."
They "help students organize thinking for writing, for
oral or visual presentations, and for problem solving."*

Howard and Sandra Black
Organizing Thinking

Notetaker
Traditional
Web

Mapmaker
United States
World
Mexico
Canada

Sequence, Cycles and Layers Labeler
Cycle
Layer
For and Against
Beginning-Middle-Ending
Sequence
Cylinder
Cause and Effect

Compare and Contrast Connector
Venn
Pyramid

Description Director
Person Portrait
Place Pyramid
Web Box
Illustration Illuminator

Graph and Grid Grappler
Large Graph
Small Graph
Dots

Fact Finder
Fact Card
Multiple Facts: List
Multiple Facts: Boxes
Multiple Facts: Categories
The Lazy L
Event Description

Time and Money Measurer
Clock Constructor
Calendar Counter
Time Liner
Currency Converter

Name _____

NOTETAKER: TRADITIONAL

Specific Topic Area: _____

Date: _____

Name of Resource: _____

Main Idea: Words/Drawing	Support: Facts, Statistics, Examples, Quotations

NOTETAKER: WEB

Write your main topic in the oval. Write the names of different parts of the main topic in the six boxes. These different parts of the main topic are called subtopics. Write supporting details for each subtopic on the lines below each box. Write the source of your information in the space provided.

Source(s) of Information: _____

_____

_____

Name _____

FACT FINDER: MULTIPLE FACTS (CATEGORIES)

Write the name of your main topic in the top box. In the remaining boxes, write the names of different parts of your main topic. These different parts of the main topic are called subtopics. On the lines below the subtopics, write the supporting details for each subtopic.

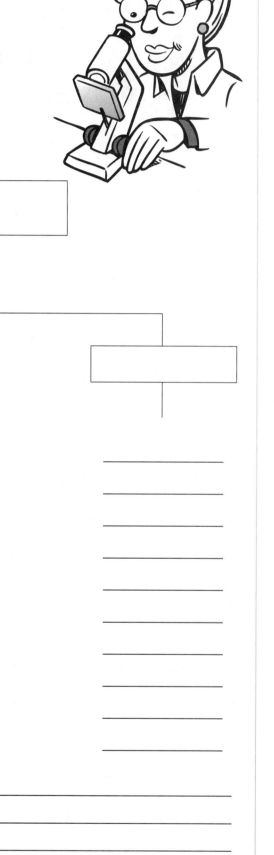

Source(s) of Information: _____

_____

_____

FACT FINDER:
MULTIPLE FACTS (LIST)

Write the page and/or date of the source for your information whether it's a book, magazine, newspaper, pamphlet, internet site or a type of multimedia.

Pg./Dt.	Source	Support Details Such as Facts, Statistics, Examples, Quotations

Name _____

FACT FINDER: MULTIPLE FACTS (BOXES)

Write or draw your main idea in the boxes on the left. Also state the source of your information. Record the supporting details in the spaces provided.

Main Idea	**Supporting Details**
	1. _____
	2. _____
Source:	3. _____
	4. _____

Supporting Details

1. _____
2. _____
3. _____
4. _____

Main Idea
Source:

Supporting Details

1. _____
2. _____
3. _____
4. _____

Main Idea
Source:

Supporting Details

1. _____
2. _____
3. _____
4. _____

Main Idea
Source:

FACT FINDER:
EVENT DESCRIPTION

Write the information describing your event in the spaces provided. Also record the source(s) of your information.

Name of event being described: _____

Who

Source: _____

What

Source: _____

When

Source: _____

Where

Source: _____

Why

Source: _____

How

Source: _____

Name _____

FACT FINDER:
FACT CARD

Record your facts on the Fact Card. Cut it out and fold. Tape the sides together.

↓ Tape or glue edges together. ↓

Front

Fact Card

Source(s) of Information: _____

Fact Topic: _____

Fact:

← Fold here

Back

Draw, diagram or chart your fact.

This Fact Card belongs to:

FACT FINDER: THE LAZY L

Write your main topic heading in the box on the left. Write the name of one part of your main topic in the box on the right. This one part of the main topic is called the subtopic. On the lines below the subtopic, write supporting details. Write the name of the source of your information in the space provided.

Subtopic

Main Topic

Supporting Details

_____

_____

_____

Source(s) of Information

_____

_____

_____

_____

_____

Subtopic

Main Topic

Supporting Details

_____

_____

_____

Source(s) of Information

_____

_____

_____

_____

_____

Name _____

DESCRIPTION DIRECTOR: PERSON PORTRAIT

Draw an illustration of the person in the center portrait frame. Record information in the remaining frames.

Family Life/Education

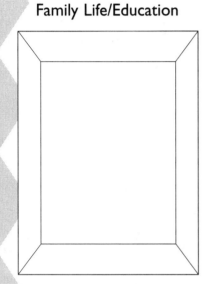

Physical Description

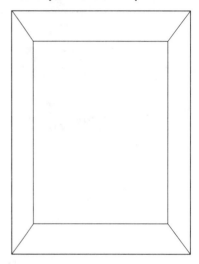

Name _____

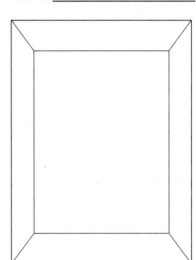

Challenges/Obstacles

Accomplishments

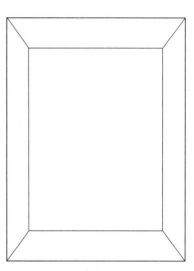

Source(s) of Information: _____

_____

Name _____

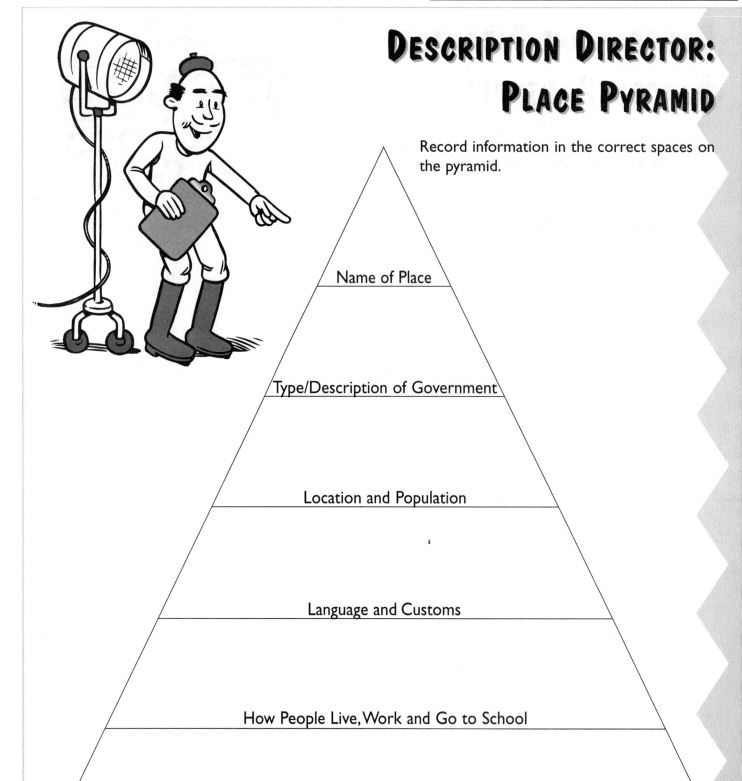

DESCRIPTION DIRECTOR: PLACE PYRAMID

Record information in the correct spaces on the pyramid.

Name of Place

Type/Description of Government

Location and Population

Language and Customs

How People Live, Work and Go to School

Climate and Geography

Source(s) of Information: _____

_____

Name _____

DESCRIPTION DIRECTOR: WEB BOX

Write the title of your main topic in the center oval. Write the names of the different parts of the main topic in the numbered ovals. (These different parts of the main topic are called subtopics.) On the numbered lines at the bottom, write supporting details about each subtopic.

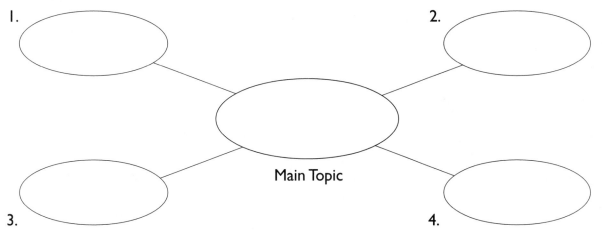

1.

2.

3.

Main Topic

4.

1. _____

_____

_____

_____

2. _____

_____

_____

_____

3. _____

_____

_____

_____

4. _____

_____

_____

_____

Source(s) of Information: _____

_____

DESCRIPTION DIRECTOR: ILLUSTRATION ILLUMINATOR

Draw an illustration of your main topic in the box, and write supporting details and the names of your sources in the spaces provided.

Fact 1: _____

Source: _____

Fact 2: _____

Source: _____

Fact 3: _____

Source: _____

Fact 4: _____

Source: _____

Fact 5: _____

Source: _____

Fact 6: _____

Source: _____

Fact 7: _____

Source: _____

Fact 8: _____

Source: _____

Name _____

COMPARE AND CONTRAST
CONNECTOR: VENN

Record your two main topic titles in the spaces provided.
Record special qualities about each topic in the large triangles.
Record how the two topics are alike in the small triangle.

Topic: _____   Topic: _____

Similarities

Source(s) of Information: _____

_____

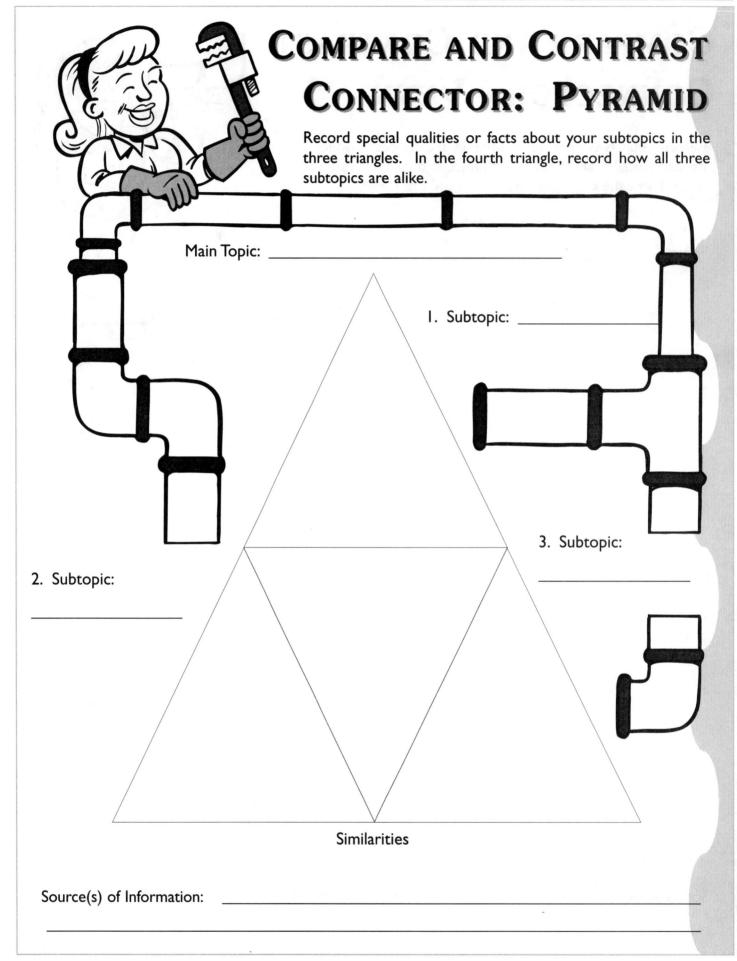

COMPARE AND CONTRAST CONNECTOR: PYRAMID

Record special qualities or facts about your subtopics in the three triangles. In the fourth triangle, record how all three subtopics are alike.

Main Topic: _____

1. Subtopic: _____

2. Subtopic:

_____

3. Subtopic:

_____

Similarities

Source(s) of Information: _____

_____

Information Processing and Organizing Roles

SEQUENCE, CYCLE AND LAYER LABELER: CYCLE

Label the different parts of the cycle and supply supporting details. Also write the source(s) of your information.

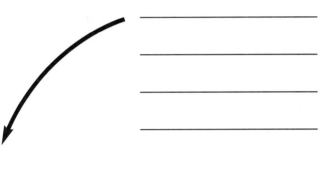

Name of Cycle

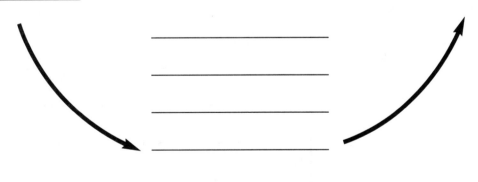

Source(s) of Information: _____

_____

Sequence, Cycle and Layer Labeler: Cylinder

If the information you've gathered can be described in layers going from bottom to top or top to bottom, use this organizer. Draw your layers in the cylinder on the left, and write your explanation on the lines provided. Also, name the source(s) of your information.

Topic: _____

Layers

Explanation

_____
_____
_____
_____
_____
_____
_____
_____
_____
_____
_____
_____
_____

Source(s) of Information: _____
_____

SEQUENCE, CYCLE AND LAYER LABELER: LAYER

If the information you've gathered can be explained according to layers, use the organizer below. Label each layer and supply supporting details in the rings. Also, tell the source(s) of your information.

Topic: _____

1. _____

2. _____

3. _____

4. _____

5. _____

Outside: _____

Source(s) of Information: _____

_____

SEQUENCE, CYCLE AND LAYER LABELER: SEQUENCE

If the information you've gathered can be described in sequence (one event leading to the next), use the organizer below. Also, name the source(s) of your information.

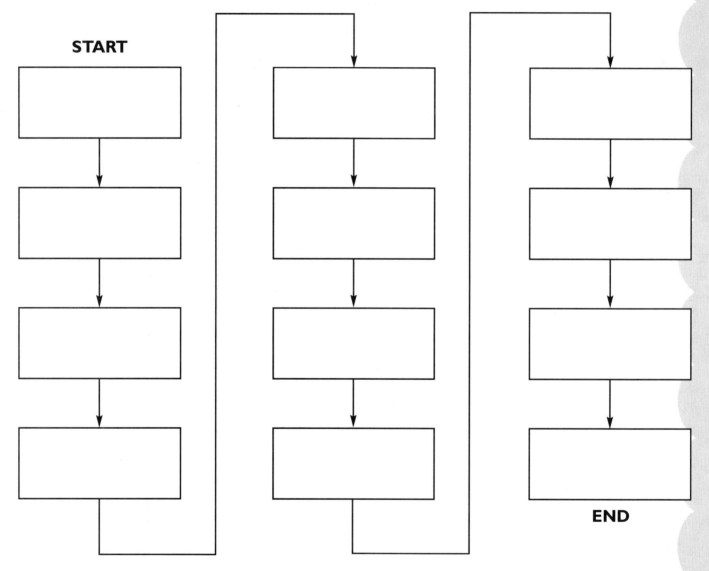

START

END

Source(s) of Information: _____

_____

Name _____

SEQUENCE, CYCLE AND LAYER LABELER: FOR AND AGAINST

In the box marked *Topic or Issue*, write the name of your topic or the issue for which you will be listing pros (for) and cons (against). For example, if the topic or issue is "the Election of Abraham Lincoln," under the *For* category list the reasons why people were in favor of electing Lincoln and in the *Against* category list the reasons why people were against his being elected.

Topic or Issue

For

Against

Source(s) of Information: _____

_____

SEQUENCE, CYCLE AND LAYER LABELER: CAUSE AND EFFECT

Write your topic or subtopic in the space provided. Next, describe the causes or reasons why in the boxes on the left, and describe the effect or results of the causes in the box on the right. If you have more than one result or effect, number them.

Topic or Subtopic: _____

Causes   **Effects**

Source(s) of Information: _____

_____

SEQUENCE, CYCLE AND LAYER LABELER: BEGINNING-MIDDLE-ENDING

In the spaces provided, describe the beginning, middle and ending of a story, person's life, a life cycle, weather pattern, building process or any type of event or process that has a beginning, a middle and an ending.

Event being described: _____

Beginning

Ending

Middle

Source(s) of Information: _____

GRAPH AND GRID GRAPPLER: SMALL GRAPH

Topic: _____

Explanation: _____

Source(s) of Information: _____

_____

GRAPH AND GRID GRAPPLER: LARGE GRAPH

Topic: _____

Explanation: _____

Source(s) of Information: _____

_____

GRAPH AND GRID
GRAPPLER: DOT

Topic: _____

Explanation: _____

  •   •   •   •   •   •   •   •   •   •   •

  •   •   •   •   •   •   •   •   •   •   •

  •   •   •   •   •   •   •   •   •   •   •

  •   •   •   •   •   •   •   •   •   •   •

  •   •   •   •   •   •   •   •   •   •   •

  •   •   •   •   •   •   •   •   •   •   •

  •   •   •   •   •   •   •   •   •   •   •

  •   •   •   •   •   •   •   •   •   •   •

  •   •   •   •   •   •   •   •   •   •   •

  •   •   •   •   •   •   •   •   •   •   •

  •   •   •   •   •   •   •   •   •   •   •

Source(s) of Information: _____

Name _____

TIME AND MONEY MEASURER: CLOCK CONSTRUCTOR

If the passage of time or the difference in time zones between cities and countries is a part of your research, record your information below.

Topic: _____

Explanation: _____

Source(s) of Information: _____

_____

Day: _____ Month: _____ Year: _____

Topic: _____

Explanation: _____

Source(s) of Information: _____

_____

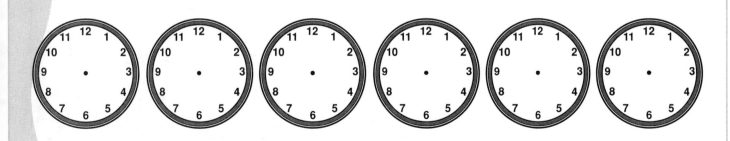

City: _____ Country: _____ Time Zone: _____

TIME AND MONEY MEASURER: CURRENCY CONVERTER

Use the American dollar as your basis for each money exchange when writing your checks below. You can convert any amount of dollars to any currency from any country in the world. To show the exchange rate, write checks in the dollar amount and in the amount of the foreign currency. Note: For a quick and easy currency converter, log onto the web at **http://www.oanda.com/cgi.-bin/ncc**.

Check No. ____

Date: _____

Pay to the Order of _____ ($) _____

_____ DOLLARS

Signature: _____

Check No. ____

Date: _____

Pay to the Order of _____ ( ) _____

Put in Currency Sign Above

_____

Name Currency Above

Signature: _____

Check No. ____

Date: _____

Pay to the Order of _____ ($) _____

_____ DOLLARS

Signature: _____

Check No. ____

Date: _____

Pay to the Order of _____ ( ) _____

Put in Currency Sign Above

_____

Name Currency Above

Signature: _____

Source(s) of Information: _____

_____

Name _____

TIME AND MONEY MEASURER: TIME LINER

Record the date above the time line in the small boxes, and write important events on the lines provided. Also, name the source(s) of your information.

Date

[ ]   [ ]   [ ]   [ ]

_____ _____ _____ _____
_____ _____ _____ _____
_____ _____ _____ _____
_____ _____ _____ _____

[ ]   [ ]   [ ]   [ ]

_____ _____ _____ _____
_____ _____ _____ _____
_____ _____ _____ _____
_____ _____ _____ _____

[ ]   [ ]   [ ]   [ ]

_____ _____ _____ _____
_____ _____ _____ _____
_____ _____ _____ _____
_____ _____ _____ _____

Source(s) of Information: _____
_____

Time and Money Measurer: Calendar Counter

Supply the month, daily dates and year before you record significant events in the boxes on your calendar. Also, name the source(s) of your information.

Topic: _____

Monthly Calendar

Month: _____   Year: _____

Sunday	Monday	Tuesday	Wednesday	Thursday	Friday	Saturday

Source(s) of Information: _____

_____

Name _____

MAPMAKER: UNITED STATES

Topic: _____

Explanation: _____

_____

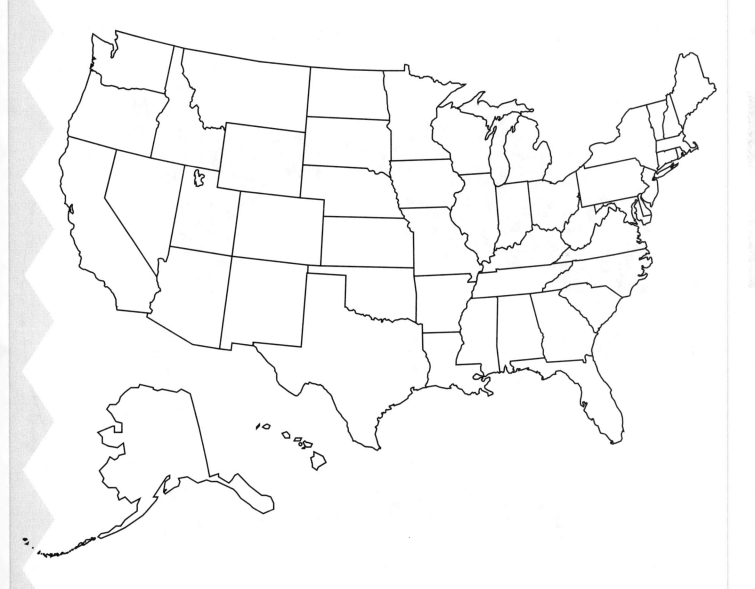

Source(s) of Information: _____

_____

MAPMAKER: WORLD

Topic: _____

Explanation: _____

_____

Source(s) of Information: _____

_____

Information Processing and Organizing Roles

Name _____

MAPMAKER: MEXICO

Topic: _____

Explanation: _____

_____

_____

_____

Source(s) of Information: _____

_____

MAPMAKER: CANADA

Topic: _____

Explanation: _____

_____

Source(s) of Information: _____

_____

Name _____

FACT FINDER: THE LAZY L

Write your main topic heading in the box on the left. Write the name of one part of your main topic in the box on the right. This one part of the main topic is called the subtopic. On the lines below the subtopic, write supporting details. Write the name of the source of your information in the space provided.

Rain Forest Animals

Main Topic

Subtopic

Poison Arrow Frog

Supporting Details

South America

eats insects

brightly colored

small enough to sit on a penny

Indians use frogs' poison on the

tips of their hunting bows.

Source(s) of Information

Rain Forest Animals by Michael Chinery

_____

Rain Forest Animals

Main Topic

Subtopic

Anaconda

Supporting Details

South America

from boa family

can grow up to 30 feet long

eats whatever it can squeeze to

death

females give birth to about 50 live

young

Source(s) of Information

Rain Forest Animals by Michael Chinery

_____

SEQUENCE, CYCLE AND LAYER LABELER: CYCLE

Label the different parts of the cycle and supply supporting details. Also write the source(s) of your information.

When water vapor cools, it forms droplets to create clouds, fog or ice crystals. When the droplets get heavy, they form precipitation, which falls to the Earth.

Precipitation (rain, sleet, hail, snow) falls to the Earth. The precipitation runs off and sinks into the ground creating groundwater.

Heat warms the water in the bodies of water, and it evapo-rates. The water changes from liquid to a gas called water vapor.

The Water Cycle
Name of Cycle

Groundwater collects and forms bodies of water such as lakes, rivers and oceans.

_____

_____

Source(s) of Information: *Geography by Anne Zeman and Kate Kelly* _____

SEQUENCE, CYCLE AND LAYER LABELER: CYLINDER

If the information you've gathered can be described in layers going from bottom to top or top to bottom, use this organizer. Draw your layers in the cylinder on the left, and write your explanation on the lines provided. Also, name the source(s) of your information.

Topic: _____ The Layers of a Rain Forest _____

Layers	**Explanation**

Emergent Layer

Canopy

Understory

Forest Floor

Emergent Layer—These giant trees are usually 130 to 180 feet tall. They have small, pointy leaves; long, straight trunks and shallow root systems.

Canopy—This is a dense part of the forest where most of the animals live. Most of the sun shines on the canopy. When it rains, the trees' leaves have "drip tips" that cause the water to run off.

Understory—This rises to 60 feet and is made up of the trunks of canopy trees, shrubs, plants and small trees.

Forest Floor—The forest floor is in deep shade and has little plant life.

Source(s) of Information: _____ *Nature's Green Umbrella by Gail Gibbons and Rain Forest by Barbara Taylor* _____

SEQUENCE, CYCLE AND LAYER LABELER: LAYER

If the information you've gathered can be explained according to layers, use the organizer below. Label each layer and supply supporting details in the rings. Also, tell the source(s) of your information.

Topic: _____ Tree Layers _____

1. Bark

2. Cambium

3. Xylem (sapwood)

4. Heartwood

5. Older wood that gives a tree strength

Carries food to all parts of the tree

Carries water and sap up from roots

Protects the tree from insects, disease, weather

Outside: Bark _____

Source(s) of Information: _____ *Discovering Trees by Douglas Florian* _____

Name _____

GRAPH AND GRID GRAPPLER: DOT

Topic: _The Big Dipper_

Explanation: _The movement of the Earth causes the constellation to appear to change its position._

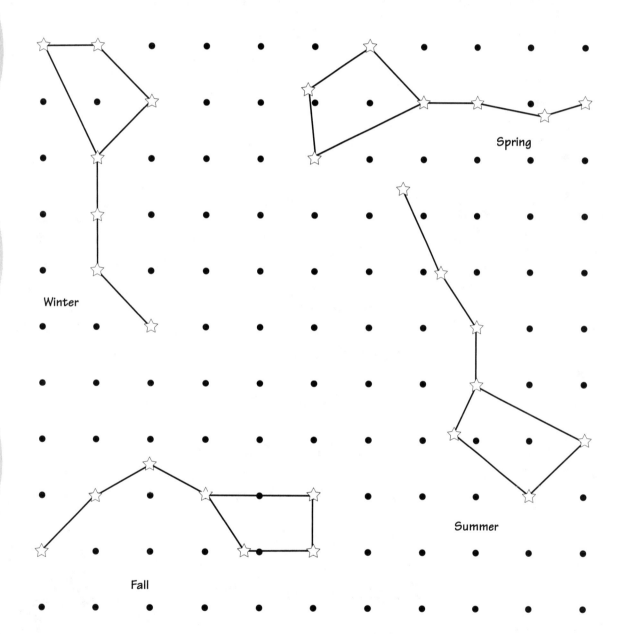

Source(s) of Information: _The Big Dipper_ by Franklyn Branley and _Find the Constellations_ by H.A. Rey

Information Presenting Roles

Group Investigation seeks to create conditions that allow students to bring their entire range of personal abilities to bear on topics of study.

Sharan & Sharan
*Expanding Cooperative Learning
Through Group Investigation*

Culture Kit Creators

Catalog Connoisseurs

Food Fanatics

Crayon Conversationalists

People Presenters

Tour Directors

Postcard Presenters

Dedicated Debaters

CULTURE KIT CREATORS

The world's people have many things in common such as families, schools, governments and holidays. A person's culture is what each person does and what each person believes about such things as his or her family, school, government or holidays. In this way, people have many things in common yet live unique, interesting lives.

To be Culture Kit Creators, follow the directions below:

1. Choose or create eight to 10 items to put into your Culture Kit box. (For example, if you are studying European countries such as Switzerland, you may want to include a road sign with directions in Italian and German since many Swiss speak these languages because Italy and Germany are Switzerland's neighbors.)

2. On the next page, in the numbered spaces for each item, list the item and explain why it is important in the culture your group researched.

3. Using the research information you have gathered, prepare a short speech for each item in which you explain the importance of the item.

4. Decorate the Culture Kit box with flags, symbols or other drawings or pictures. Make sure you explain these decorations as part of your presentation.

5. Practice your group presentation.

   - Divide the items and speeches among group members.
   - Members should either memorize their speeches or use note cards.
   - Practice removing each item from the box and placing it on display at the end of each speech.
   - Plan a brief introduction and conclusion to your presentation.

Special Note: You can turn the Culture Kit into a Time Capsule Kit by including only items from a particular time period such as America in the 50s, France in the 1700s or China during the Ming Dynasty.

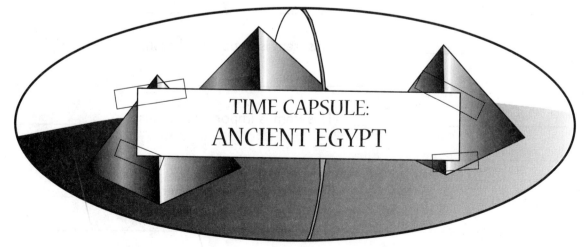

TIME CAPSULE:
ANCIENT EGYPT

CULTURE KIT CREATORS

Write the name of each item in your Culture Kit or Time Capsule, and explain why it is important in the culture or time period you've researched.

Item 1: _____ This item is important because _____

_____.

Item 2: _____ This item is important because _____

_____.

Item 3: _____ This item is important because _____

_____.

Item 4: _____ This item is important because _____

_____.

Item 5: _____ This item is important because _____

_____.

Item 6: _____ This item is important because _____

_____.

Item 7: _____ This item is important because _____

_____.

Item 8: _____ This item is important because _____

_____.

Item 9: _____ This item is important because _____

_____.

Item 10: _____ This item is important because _____

_____.

Names _____

PEOPLE PRESENTERS

Your role as People Presenters is to write and perform a brief play describing a famous person's life. Based on your research, this person could be anyone such as an inventor, explorer, scientist, author, artist, musician, entrepreneur, world leader, religious figure, military leader or even a character from a book.

The play should be written and performed in first person with different group members playing the famous person at different stages in his or her life.

To be People Presenters, follow the directions below.

1. Using your research information, create a detailed time line of the person's life. Be sure to include names of important people and places as well as the person's accomplishments and struggles.

2. Using the time line, complete the planning sheets your teacher gives you. Special Note: When listing the props you will need for your play, list any tables and chairs as well as personal items such as reading glasses or books.

3. Using your completed planning sheet, write the script for your play. Make sure you write a brief introduction to your play.

4. Rehearse your play. Each group member should perform his or her part and allow the other group members to offer suggestions and encouragement.

5. If possible, videotape one of your rehearsals so you can see your performance. Make any changes necessary after viewing the videotape.

6. During your final rehearsal, make sure you rehearse with all of your props and costume pieces.

Options to the first person performance include:

• Acting out important scenes from the person's life using a narrator to provide details between the scenes.

• Using a "this-is-your-life" approach and creating several scenes where significant people from the person's life tell about events that occurred. The narrator introduces each person.

People Presenters Planning Sheet

Scene 1

1. What will I need to wear in order to show my audience when and where this person lived?

_____

2. How will I speak in order to show this person's age? _____

_____

What kind of accent or special words or phrases will I use? _____

_____

3. What kinds of props will I need? _____

_____

4. What important events in this person's life should be included in this part of the play? _____

_____

Scene 2

1. What will I wear in order to show my audience when and where this person lived? _____

_____

2. How will I speak in order to show this person's age? _____

_____

What kind of accent or special words or phrases will I use? _____

_____

3. What kinds of props will I need? _____

_____

4. What important events in this person's life should be included in this part of the play?_____

_____

Names _____

People Presenters Planning Sheet

Scene 3

1. What will I need to wear in order to show my audience when and where this person lived?

   _____

2. How will I speak in order to show this person's age? _____

   _____

   What kind of accent or special words or phrases will I use? _____

   _____

3. What kinds of props will I need? _____

   _____

4. What important events in this person's life should be included in this part of the play? _____

   _____

Scene 4

1. What will I wear in order to show my audience when and where this person lived? _____

   _____

2. How will I speak in order to show this person's age? _____

   _____

   What kind of accent or special words or phrases will I use? _____

   _____

3. What kinds of props will I need? _____

   _____

4. What important events in this person's life should be included in this part of the play? _____

   _____

CRAYON CONVERSATIONALISTS

Your role as Crayon Conversationalists is to create a presentation that includes illustrating or drawing while talking to your audience about your research information. Below are some ways you might want to complete this role.

- Group members take turns drawing portions of a map and explaining the different geography, cities, rivers, populations, vegetation and historical sites of a specific country, state or province.

- Group members take turns drawing different plants or animals and explaining the features of each.

- Group members take turns drawing portions of a life cycle, weather pattern or ecological system.

- Group members take turns drawing an illustrated time line and explaining the historical events and significant people.

- Group members take turns illustrating the beginning, middle and ending of a movement such as the Civil Rights movement.

- Group members take turns drawing an illustration of government systems and the election processes used in those systems.

- Group members take turns drawing portraits of significant people and explaining their accomplishments.

To be Crayon Conversationalists, follow the directions below.

1. Discuss the type of presentation you would like to create. On the back of this sheet, list all the possible people, places, events, steps and categories of information that might be included in your presentation.

2. Choose the most important information you wish to include in your presentation and make a list. (Each group member should illustrate and explain one or two items for your presentation. Your crayon presentation shouldn't include more than 10 illustrated items if possible.)

3. Your teacher will give you planning sheets. On your planning sheets, arrange in order the items among the group members.

4. Each group member should draw a brief sketch of what he or she plans to illustrate during his or her portion of the presentation.

5. Finally, group members should work together to write brief notes in the spaces provided on the planning sheet about what should be said during the illustration of each item.

6. Group members should practice taking turns illustrating their portion of the presentation and explaining their item(s). During rehearsal, the group should finalize the order of each item, the information in each speech and the illustration.

Special Note: Groups do not have to use crayons although they may if they wish. Different colored chalk or markers can be used on chalkboards, dry-eraser boards or rolls of newsprint.

Names _____

Crayon Conversationalists
Planning Sheet

Item Description/Significance

_____

_____

_____

_____

_____

_____

_____

_____

_____

Illustration

Item Description/Significance

_____

_____

_____

_____

_____

_____

_____

_____

Illustration

POSTCARD PRESENTERS

Your role as Postcard Presenters is to create a series of post-cards based on the research information you've gathered. You can create a series of postcards that describe many topics such as:

- plants and animals from different regions of the world
- land formations and bodies of water such as major rivers of the United States or mountain ranges around the world

- battlefields and other historical sites
- birthplaces of famous people
- parks, museums and cities
- planets, stars and solar systems

In addition, you can create postcards that seem to come from ages past. For example, you could create a series of postcards as if they had come from someone traveling west on the Oregon Trail or create a series of postcards as if they had been written by someone like Marco Polo as he traveled to the Far East.

To be Postcard Presenters, follow the directions below.

1. Create a list of 20 possible topics for your series of postcards.

2. Discuss the pros and cons of each item on your list, and then select 10 to 12 items for your postcards.

3. Your teacher will give you postcard sheets to use for your series of postcards. Before using these sheets, however, create "mock-ups" or first drafts of each of your postcards on blank pieces of paper. To create your "mock-up" do the following:

    1. Draw a sketch of the item you wish to appear on the front of your postcard.

    2. Write a detailed description of the item which will appear on the back of the card.

    3. Decide what type of stamp to draw. (You can access images of stamps from around the world by typing in the words *postage stamps* after logging onto the AltaVista search engine at **http://www.altavista.com**.)

    4. Write an address.

Make sure you divide the responsibilities for the postcards among all group members.

4. Review the mock-ups of your postcards. Discuss each sketch and decide if you wish to make changes. Read each description. Check to make sure facts in the description as well as the spelling and wording are correct.

5. Create the final draft of each of your postcards using the postcard sheets your teacher has given you. (You may want to word process your description and then cut it out and tape it or paste it onto the postcard.)

6. Draw a map to go along with your postcards. Practice your group presentation. (Each group member should tell about one or two postcards and explain where the item can be found on the map.) Make sure your presentation has an introduction and conclusion.

Names _____

POSTCARD PRESENTERS

Front of Postcard: Draw picture.

Fold Here →

Stamp

Write picture description here.

Address

_____

_____

_____

_____

Back of Postcard

TOUR DIRECTORS

Your role as Tour Directors is to take your audience on a tour of the house, building, park, forest, desert, city, state, province, country, ocean, river, sea, continent, planet or solar system you've researched. You can take your audience on a tour of historical ages and places as well as future or imaginary places. (You can tour any place from the inside of a tornado to the tomb of King Tut!) As part of your tour, you will provide your audience with informative brochures.

To be Tour Directors, follow the directions below.

1. Create a list of 10 to 15 places you may want to include on your tour.

2. Discuss the pros and cons of each place and choose six to eight. (Each group member will present two or three places during your tour presentation.)

3. Your teacher will give you brochure planning sheets to use to create your tour brochures. Use these sheets to create "mock-ups" or first drafts of each of the brochures. To create your "mock-up" of each brochure, do the following:

   1. Divide the responsibilities for the brochures among group members.

   2. Fold the planning sheet into thirds as illustrated on page 107.

   3. Draw a sketch of the place on the cover.

   4. On the remaining folds, write a description of the place based on your research.

   5. On the back of the tri-fold, write the name of your tour company.

4. Review the mock-ups of your brochures. Decide if you wish to make any changes in the sketches or descriptions. Make sure the descriptions are correct, and check spelling and wording.

5. Create the final draft of each of your brochures using another set of brochure sheets or folding blank pieces of paper into thirds. (You may want to word process your descriptions and then cut them out and paste or tape them onto your brochures.)

6. Draw a map to go along with your tour brochures. (If you are giving a tour of a house or building such as the White House, create a simple blueprint of the house or building telling where each room is.)

7. Practice your group presentation using your tour brochures. Each group member should tell about one or two places and explain where each can be found on the map or blueprint. Remember to have an introduction and conclusion to your tour.

8. As each group member practices his or her part of the tour, other group members should offer suggestions and encouragement. (If possible, videotape one of your rehearsals so you can see each group member's performance. Make changes if necessary.)

Names _____

TOUR DIRECTORS' BROCHURE PLANNING SHEET

| Illustration | Front Page |
| Fold Here → |
| Description | Middle Page |
| Fold Here → |
| Description | Last Page |

CATALOG CONNOISSEURS

As Catalog Connoisseurs, it is your role to create a catalog complete with illustrations and informative descriptions. Using the research information you've gathered, you may want to create a catalog of such items as clothing, modes of transportation, household furniture and utensils, as well as toys, recreational equipment, medicines and food. Of course, these items come from the country, culture, time period, author or famous person you have researched. Catalog items for science-related topics could include scientific equipment, plants, animals, medicines and health items such as vitamins and exercise equipment and programs.

To be Catalog Connoisseurs, follow the directions below.

1. On the back of this sheet, make a list of 20 to 25 possible items for your catalog.

2. Discuss each item. Think about the following:

   • During your research, did you discover the item to be unique, necessary or important?

   • Do you have enough research information to write an informative description of the item?

   • Is someone in your group able to draw the item or get a picture for the catalog?

3. Choose 10 to 15 items to include in your catalog.

4. Divide the responsibilities so each group member is either writing, illustrating or doing both.

5. Create a first draft or "mock-up" of your catalog with brief sketches and written descriptions.

6. Using the catalog sheets that your teacher gives you, create the final draft of your catalog. Proofread your catalog and make any corrections.

7. Create a front cover, back cover and order form for your catalog. Staple or bind your covers and pages together.

8. Practice taking turns talking about the items in your catalog. During your group presentation, you will need to walk around the room showing the catalog, or make a set of overhead transparencies so the class can see each catalog item as you discuss it. In your presentation:

   • tell the audience what the item is

   • tell why the item is important, unique or necessary

   • tell how the item is used

   • tell the cost of the item if that is included in your catalog

Special Note: If you want to include prices in your catalog in dollars as well as foreign currency, you can log onto **http://www.oanda.com/cgi-bin/ncc** to get an accurate currency exchange rate.

Names _____

CATALOG CONNOISSEURS

Item

_____

_____

_____

_____

_____

_____

_____

_____

_____

_____

Item

_____

_____

_____

_____

_____

_____

_____

_____

_____

_____

FOOD FANATICS

Your role as Food Fanatics is to create a presentation that demonstrates what your research information has revealed about the importance of food. Some suggestions of ways you might want to organize your research information include:

- foods eaten in different countries
- foods eaten on special occasions or holidays
- foods eaten during different historical periods
- foods that are nutritionally "good" or "bad"
- where certain foods are grown in the world
- foods used as medicines
- how certain foods are grown
- how hybrid foods are created
- the use of pesticides and herbicides on foods and their effects
- the types of plants that produce certain foods
- food production and distribution around the world
- food storage systems
- the effect of weather on food production
- the types of food available in different restaurants and grocery stores around the world

To be Food Fanatics follow the directions below.

1. Discuss the topics above and add others of your own based on your group's research.

2. Decide which topic area your group would like to use in its presentation.

3. Decide on a presentation method. Choose from the suggestions below, or create a presentation method of your own.

- Create a restaurant menu complete with illustrations, delicious descriptions and prices.
- Create a grocery store shopping trip using a bilingual grocery list.
- Create a map showing where certain foods are grown.
- Create charts and graphs that show food production.
- Create a set of small posters with illustrations of plants on one side and the medicines created from the plants on the reverse side.
- Cook or bake different dishes eaten in other countries.
- Create a display of foods that are nutritionally "good" or "bad."
- Write a play that explains how weather affects food production.
- Stage a debate about the pros and cons of pesticide and herbicide use.

4. Divide the responsibilities among group members. Use the Food Fanatics Planning Sheet to help you plan, organize and carry out your project.

5. Create your poster, play, display, etc., using your planning sheet as a guide.

6. Rehearse your presentation.

Names _____

Food Fanatics Planning Sheet

1. Title of presentation

   _____

   _____

2. Tell what you are going to do.

   _____

   _____

3. Tell the materials you will need.

   _____

   _____

4. Tell the steps you will follow.

   _____

   _____

5. Tell any problems you might have.

   _____

   _____

6. Tell how you will solve any problems.

   _____

   _____

DEDICATED DEBATERS

Your role as Dedicated Debaters is to present the positive or "pros" of one side of an issue or to present the negative or "cons" of the same issue. Some topics or issues can be seen in both positive and negative ways. In other words, there is strong research information that supports both sides of the issue. Some topics where information supports both sides include:

- controlling the information that gets onto the internet
- using vouchers to allow students to choose their school
- requiring students to do community service before they graduate
- requiring seat belts on all school buses and vehicles
- outlawing the death penalty
- using curfew laws to attempt to reduce vandalism and other crimes
- requiring teens to have a driver's permit for one year before getting a permanent driver's license

To be Dedicated Debaters, follow the directions below.

1. Review the information you've gathered in support of your side of the issue.

2. Choose the most valuable information, and complete the debate planning sheet your teacher gives you.

3. Group members help Speakers 1 and 2 prepare their speeches. Each two-minute speech should include information in support of your side of the topic and also the names of resources where you got your information. Speakers 1 and 2 should practice their speeches as Speakers 3 and 4 assist with suggestions and encouragement.

4. Group members review the information they've gathered that does not support their side of the issue.

5. Group members prepare possible audience questions based on the above information. (The class audience is the opposing "team.")

6. Using their research information, members prepare answers to the questions.

7. Members help prepare Speaker 3 by asking questions and having him or her respond using research information.

8. Group members prepare Speaker 4's conclusion speech and assist Speaker 4 with rehearsing his or her speech.

9. During the actual debate, group members should be well-prepared by having their research information readily available to assist Speaker 3 during the question-and-answer period.

Special Note: Your teacher may have questions prepared to give to audience members.

Names _____

DEDICATED DEBATERS
PLANNING SHEET

Debate Topic Statement: _____

Speaker 1: Main Points (2 mins.)

1. _____

Resources _____

2. _____

Resources _____

3. _____

Resources _____

4. _____

Resources _____

Speaker 2: Main Points (2 mins.)

1. _____

Resources _____

2. _____

Resources _____

3. _____

Resources _____

4. _____

Resources _____

Speaker 3: Possible Questions

1. _____
2. _____
3. _____
4. _____
5. _____
6. _____

Speaker 3: Answers and Resources (2 mins.)

1. _____
2. _____
3. _____
4. _____
5. _____
6. _____

Speaker 4: Main Points in Conclusion (2 mins.)

1. _____

Resources _____

2. _____

Resources _____

3. _____

Resources _____

4. _____

Resources _____

Assessment Rubrics and Checklists

Group Investigation is particularly effective in increasing higher level cognitive abilities among students.

Spencer Kagan
Cooperative Learning

Assessment

Assessing the group research process and project can be manageable and fair if three components comprise the assessment:

- Students are aware of how they will be evaluated at each stage in the research process and project.

- Assessment devices are consistent with the process and materials that are to be evaluated.

- Each student's overall grade for the entire project is based on a combination of individual and group grades.

First, students should have copies of each of the assessment forms that you plan to use during the research project and process. To accomplish this, an explanation as to when each assessment device should be discussed with students is provided with each of the 10 steps in the introductory material.

Secondly, each of the assessment forms in this book is based on checklist rubrics and Likert-type scales that provide a wide variety of evaluation options. In addition, some of the assessment forms assess group work while others evaluate individual student contributions.

Because the assessment forms include group as well as individual evaluations, you are able to base each student's grade on a combination of grades and not just one group grade or all individual grades–which would defeat the interdependence aspect necessary for successful group projects. A suggested combination for computing each student's grade follows.

Using a value system of your choosing, combine the following evaluations:

- One group session evaluation (planning, sharing or preparing). Since it will be nearly impossible for you to evaluate every group during planning, sharing and preparing sessions, designate which groups you will evaluate during each of the sessions so you will be able to complete at least two different group evaluations during each of the sessions.

- One or two individual evaluations (based on Steps 4 and 6). It may be possible for you to evaluate each student as he or she completes his or her Information Gathering Role. It may also be possible for you to evaluate each student as he or she completes his or her combination of graphic organizers. However, if you are not able to evaluate each student twice, then divide the number of individual evaluations between Steps 4 and 6.

- One or two student evaluations (Steps 4-8 and Step 10). You may wish to select, at random, student evaluations to include in the overall grade. You may want to offer automatic points for a completed evaluation or base your grade or points on the thoroughness and thoughtfulness of the student evaluation.

- One group presentation evaluation (based on Step 9). Each group presentation should be given a group grade and included as a portion of the student's overall grade.

By combining the four evaluation components above, you should be able to arrive at a fair individual student grade. At the same time, the evaluation process should be manageable for you.

Teacher Evaluation: Group Planning Session (Step 3)

Group Members' Names: _____ Date _____

Task Achievement	**Yes**	**No**	**Somewhat**

1. The group considered several topics before deciding upon one.   ____ ____ ____

Comments: _____

2. The group discussed the Topic Breakout Sheet.   ____ ____ ____

Comments: _____

3. The group made any necessary revisions to the
   Topic Breakout Sheet.   ____ ____ ____

Comments: _____

4. The group completed its What-Want-Where Sheet.   ____ ____ ____

Comments: _____

5. The group completed its Planning Session Sheet.   ____ ____ ____

Comments: _____

6. The group placed its Planning Sheet on display and
   recorded its due date on the classroom calendar.   ____ ____ ____

Comments: _____

Group Functioning

1. Group members didn't waste a lot of time and stayed on task.

   Always   Frequently   Often   Sometimes   Seldom   Never

2. Group members paid attention to one another by:

   asking questions

   Always   Frequently   Often   Sometimes   Seldom   Never

   listening to one another

   Always   Frequently   Often   Sometimes   Seldom   Never

   looking at one another

   Always   Frequently   Often   Sometimes   Seldom   Never

3. Group members let everyone contribute ideas–not just one or two people.

   Always   Frequently   Often   Sometimes   Seldom   Never

4. Group members got along with one another.

   Always   Frequently   Often   Sometimes   Seldom   Never

STUDENT EVALUATION: GROUP PLANNING SESSION (STEP 3)

Student's Name: _____ Date: _____

Directions: Carefully read each item and answer to the best of your ability. Use complete sentences when writing any responses.

How the Group Did	Yes	No	Somewhat
1. We completed all of the work.			
We selected a topic.	____	____	____
We completed the Topic Breakout Sheet.	____	____	____
We completed the What-Want-Where Chart.	____	____	____
We completed the Planning Session Sheet.	____	____	____
We displayed the Planning Sheet and date.	____	____	____

If not, explain why not. _____

2. We all got a chance to contribute our ideas.	____	____	____

If not, explain why not. _____

3. We all got along with one another.	____	____	____

If not, explain why not. _____

How I Did in the Group
Check each item you did in today's group.

_____ contributed my ideas

_____ asked questions

_____ answered questions

_____ followed directions

_____ listened while others spoke

_____ smiled

_____ did not complain

_____ took on the role of leader

_____ helped others stay on task

_____ helped resolve conflict

_____ encouraged everyone to contribute

_____ checked to see if the group agreed on ideas

_____ did my fair share of the work

_____ tried to have fun but still got the work done

_____ did not use negative terms like *dumb* or *stupid*

_____ looked at other members while they spoke

_____ added to other people's ideas and suggestions

_____ did not interrupt others while they spoke

_____ did not distract other members

_____ wrote down ideas for What-Want-Where Chart

_____ wrote down group's plan on Planning Session Sheet

Teacher Evaluation: Information Gathering (Step 4)

Student's Name: _____ Date: _____

Check here if student _____ changed roles _____ added roles

Student's role(s):   Internet Investigator   Periodical Person   Encyclopedia Explorer

Atlas Analyzer   Pamphlet Person   Book Browser   Newspaper Notetaker

Dictionary Detective   In-Depth Interviewer   Multimedia Messenger   Almanac Attacker

1. While completing his or her role, the student asked questions and/or asked for help when necessary.

    Always   Frequently   Often   Sometimes   Seldom   Never

2. The student used his or her time productively.

    Always   Frequently   Often   Sometimes   Seldom   Never

3. The student interacted and shared information with group members when necessary and appropriate.

    Always   Frequently   Often   Sometimes   Seldom   Never

4. The student did not give up when problems occurred or when resource information wasn't readily available.

    Always   Frequently   Often   Sometimes   Seldom   Never

5. The student kept his or her research information in his or her project folder and appeared to be organized.

    Always   Frequently   Often   Sometimes   Seldom   Never

Evaluation of Completed Information Gathering Role Sheets

	Excellent	Good	Fair	Poor
Completeness of Role Sheets				
Documenting Resources				
Variety of Resources Used				

118

Student Evaluation: Information Gathering (Step 4)

Student's Name: _____ Date: _____

Directions: Carefully read each item and answer to the best of your ability.

My Information Gathering Role(s) was_____.

I **did** or **did not** (circle one) change roles during this portion of the research project.

Of the roles listed above, I added the role of _____ to my original choice.

1. I paid attention during the mini lesson designed to teach me how to find research resources.

    Always   *Frequently*   *Often*   *Sometimes*   *Seldom*   *Never*

2. While I was completing my role, I asked questions when I needed to.

    Always   *Frequently*   *Often*   *Sometimes*   *Seldom*   *Never*

3. I shared resource information with other group members in a timely and appropriate manner.

    Always   *Frequently*   *Often*   *Sometimes*   *Seldom*   *Never*

4. I used my time productively.

    Always   *Frequently*   *Often*   *Sometimes*   *Seldom*   *Never*

5. I kept all my resource information in my project folder.

    Always   *Frequently*   *Often*   *Sometimes*   *Seldom*   *Never*

6. The most difficult part of this role was _____

_____

_____

7. The most interesting part of this role was _____

_____

_____

8. During my information gathering, I found information not only on the subtopics I was researching, but I also found information that helped the following group members: _____

_____

_____

TEACHER EVALUATION: GROUP SHARING SESSION (STEP 5)

Group Members' Names: _____ Date: _____

Task Achievement	**Yes**	**No**	**Somewhat**
1. Members had their Planning Sheet and their What-Want-Where Charts with them.	____	____	____

Comments: _____

2. Members discussed the research information they had gathered and how the information related to the subtopics on the Planning Sheet.	____	____	____

Comments: _____

3. If members agreed, they made subtopic changes on the group's planning sheets.	____	____	____

Comments: _____

4. Members exchanged information and resource titles that involved other members' research subtopics.	____	____	____

Comments: _____

5. Members reviewed their What-Want-Where chart and made suggestions about where to find additional research.	____	____	____

Comments: _____

6. Members agreed on a date for their preparing session and recorded the date on the classroom research calendar.	____	____	____

Comments: _____

Group Functioning

1. Group members took the necessary materials to the session.

    Always   *Frequently*   *Often*   *Sometimes*   *Seldom*   *Never*

2. Group members were helpful and supportive of one another.

    Always   *Frequently*   *Often*   *Sometimes*   *Seldom*   *Never*

3. Group members were able to reach agreement about subtopics.

    Always   *Frequently*   *Often*   *Sometimes*   *Seldom*   *Never*

4. Group members freely contributed ideas and did not let one or two people dominate.

    Always   *Frequently*   *Often*   *Sometimes*   *Seldom*   *Never*

Student Evaluation: Group Sharing Session (Step 5)

Group Members' Names: _____ Date: _____

Task Achievement	**Yes**	**No**	**Somewhat**
1. Members had their Planning Sheets, their What-Want-Where Charts and their research information with them during the group discussion.	____	____	____
2. Members discussed the subtopics and how the information the group gathered related to them.	____	____	____
3. Members exchanged information and resource titles with other members.	____	____	____
4. Members tried to help one another by giving suggestions about where to find additional research information.	____	____	____
5. Everyone got a chance to contribute ideas—not just one or two people.	____	____	____

How I Did in the Group

1. The most important contribution I made to the group was _____

_____

_____

2. One thing I could have done better in the group was _____

_____

_____

3. My role in the group was primarily as the person who:

_____	got the group organized	_____	asked questions so everyone understood the discussion
_____	made suggestions	_____	helped everyone get along
_____	started the discussion	_____	other (Explain.) _____
_____	got the materials the group needed		_____
_____	got everyone to agree		_____
_____	got everyone to participate		_____

Teacher Evaluation: Information Evaluating, Processing and Organizing (Step 6)

Student's Name: _____ Date: _____

The circled organizers are the ones this student used during this portion of the research process. The code that appears in the blank next to the organizer indicates the degree to which the organizer was used appropriately and how completely it was done. The numbers indicate:

1 = Excellent   2 = Good   3 = Fair   4 = Poor

Students who completed more than one copy of the same organizer receive a rating score for each one.

Sequence, Cycles and Layers Labeler

_____ Cycle

_____ Sequence

_____ Layer

_____ Cylinder

_____ For and Against

_____ Cause and Effect

_____ Beginning-Middle-Ending

Notetaker

_____ Traditional

_____ Web

Description Director

_____ Person Portrait

_____ Place Pyramid

_____ Web Box

_____ Illustration Illuminator

Compare and Contrast Connector

_____ Venn

_____ Pyramid

Graph and Grid Grappler

_____ Large Graph

_____ Small Graph

_____ Dots

Fact Finder

_____ Fact Card

_____ Multiple Facts: List

_____ Multiple Facts: Boxes

_____ Multiple Facts: Categories

_____ The Lazy L

_____ Event Description

I observed the following while this student processed and organized his or her information:

_____

_____

_____

122

STUDENT EVALUATION: INFORMATION EVALUATING, PROCESSING AND ORGANIZING (STEP 6)

Student's Name: _____ Date: _____

Directions: Carefully read each item and answer to the best of your ability.

The subtopic(s) I am researching is _____

The graphic organizers I found most useful were _____

_____ because _____

_____

_____

I tried using the following graphic organizer(s): _____

_____, but I gave up using it/them because

_____

_____

The graphic organizers were **easy   difficult** for me to use because _____

_____

_____

Using graphic organizers helped me be more organized about my research information.

    Yes   *No*   *Somewhat*

Using graphic organizers helped me remember what kind of research information I'd gathered.

    Yes   *No*   *Somewhat*

Using graphic organizers made it easier to share research information with my group.

    Yes   *No*   *Somewhat*

Using graphic organizers helped me better understand the research information I'd gathered.

    Yes   *No*   *Somewhat*

TEACHER EVALUATION: PREPARING SESSION AND GROUP PREPARATION (STEPS 7 AND 8)

Group Members' Names: _____ Date: _____

Task Achievement	**Yes**	**No**	**Somewhat**
1. The group identified the special talents of each group member.	____	____	____
2. The group discussed the research information they had gathered and suggested possible group presentations.	____	____	____
3. The group discussed the pros and cons of suggested presentations and agreed upon one.	____	____	____
4. The group divided the responsibilities of the presentation project among group members.	____	____	____
5. The group completed its preparing sheet and recorded its presentation date on the classroom research calendar.	____	____	____

Group Preparation: Group Functioning

1. The group met in its designated area.

   Always   *Frequently*   *Often*   *Sometimes*   *Seldom*   *Never*

2. The group acted responsibly by keeping track of its materials and completed work.

   Always   *Frequently*   *Often*   *Sometimes*   *Seldom*   *Never*

3. Group members stayed with the group and didn't wander around the room or disturb others.

   Always   *Frequently*   *Often*   *Sometimes*   *Seldom*   *Never*

4. The group regularly met its goals as recorded on its Daily Group Progress Log.

   Always   *Frequently*   *Often*   *Sometimes*   *Seldom*   *Never*

5. Each group member appeared to be doing his or her fair share of the work.

   Always   *Frequently*   *Often*   *Sometimes*   *Seldom*   *Never*

6. Group members were helpful and supportive of one another.

   Always   *Frequently*   *Often*   *Sometimes*   *Seldom*   *Never*

Additional Comments: _____

_____

_____

_____

_____

Student Evaluation: Preparing Session and Group Preparation (Steps 7 and 8)

Student's Name: _____ Date: _____

Directions: Carefully read each item and answer to the best of your ability.

Task Achievement   Yes   No   Somewhat

1. The group was fair in identifying the talents of the different
   group members.   ____   ____   ____

Comments: _____

2. The group was fair in dividing up the responsibilities of the
   presentation among group members.   ____   ____   ____

Comments: _____

3. Everyone got a chance to tell what was good or bad about the
   suggested group presentations.   ____   ____   ____

Comments: _____

4. All group members agreed upon the chosen group presentation.   ____   ____   ____

Comments: _____

How I Did in the Group

Below is a list of all the big and little things I did to help create and prepare for the project presentation.

1. _____

2. _____

3. _____

4. _____

5. _____

6. _____

7. _____

8. _____

9. _____

10. _____

Teacher Evaluation: Group Presentation (Step 9)

Group Members' Names: _____ Date _____

Information Presenting Role: _____

	Overall Presentation	Research Information	Materials Created/Used	Group Responsibilities
Excellent	All members knew their parts. Significant evidence of rehearsal and preparation.	An abundance of relevant research information included in the presentation.	Materials created/ used were complete, appropriate and carefully done.	Every group member had an equal part in the presentation.
Good	Members knew their parts but some lack of rehearsal and preparation evident.	Large amount of research included in the presentation.	Not all materials were carefully or completely done. All not appropriate.	Evident that not every member had equal responsibilities.
Fair	Not all members knew their parts. Presentation did not go smoothly.	Some research information used. Several missed opportunities.	Materials showed little effort. Some incomplete and missing.	Presentation was dominated by two people.
Poor	Lack of rehearsal and preparation evident.	Very little research information included.	Few materials created or used in presentation.	Presentation was dominated by one person.

Student Evaluation: Group Project Review (Step 10)

Student's Name: _____ Date: _____

Directions: Answer each question to the best of your ability. The information you provide will help make future group research projects even better. Thank you for your honest, thoughtful answers!

1. Tell what were the best and worst parts of each of the different types of roles used in the project.

   Information Gathering Roles (Internet Investigator, Newspaper Notetaker, etc.)

   Best: _____

   Worst: _____

   Information Processing and Organizing Roles (Graphic Organizers)

   Best: _____

   Worst: _____

   Information Presenting Roles (Culture Kit Creators, Postcard Presenters, etc.)

   Best: _____

   Worst: _____

2. The most enjoyable part of the group research project was _____

   _____

3. I **would   would not**   want to participate in another group research project because _____

   _____

4. To improve the group research project, the one important thing I would change or do differently

   would be _____.

   This change would make the project better because _____

   _____

5. I learned **as much as   not as much as   even more than**   I would have learned about my

   topic had I done the research alone because _____

6. The most important thing I learned about being a group member was _____

   _____

Bibliography

Abrami, Philip C. et.al. *Classroom Connections: Understanding and Using Cooperative Learning*. New York: Harcourt Brace: 1995.

Bellanca, James. *The Cooperative Think Tank II*. Palatine: Skylight Publishing, 1992.

Black, Howard and Sandra. *Organizing Thinking: Book II*. Pacific Grove: Critical Thinking Press & Software, 1990.

Boyles, Nancy. *The Learning Differences Sourcebook*. Los Angeles: Lowell House Contemporary Books, 1997.

Cohen, Elizabeth G. *Designing Groupwork: Strategies for the Heterogenous Classroom*. New York: Teachers College Press, 1994.

Gardner, Howard. *Frames of Mind*. New York: Basic Books, 1983.

Gralla, Preston. *Online Kids: A Young Surfer's Guide to Cyberspace*. John Wiley and Sons, Inc., 1996.

Humphreys, B., R.T. Johnson, and D.W. Johnson (1982). "Effects of Cooperative, Competitive and Individualistic Learning on Students' Achievement in Science Class." *Journal of Research in Science Teaching*. 19, 351-356.

Johnson, D.W., and R.T. Johnson. *Learning Together and Alone: Cooperative, Competitive and Individualistic Learning*. Englewood: Prentice Hall, 1987.

_____. (1981). "Effects of Cooperative and Individualistic Learning Experiences on Interethnic Interaction." *Journal of Educational Psychology*, 73, 444-449.

Johnson, D.W., L. Skon, and R.T. Johnson. (1980). "Effects of Cooperative, Competitive and Individualistic Conditions on Children's Problem-Solving Performance." *American Educational Research Journal,* 17, 83-93.

Johnson, R.T., D.W. Johnson, and J. Rynders. (1981). "Effects of Cooperative, Competitive and Individualistic Experiences on Self-Esteem of Handicapped and Non-Handicapped Students." *Journal of Psychology,* 108, 31-34.

Kagan, Spencer. *Cooperative Learning*. San Juan Capistrano: Kagan Cooperative Learning, 1992.

Lyman, Lawrence, Harvey Foyle, and Tara Azwell. *Cooperative Learning in the Elementary Classroom*. National Educational Association Library Publication, 1993.

McInerney, Claire. *Tracking the Facts: How to Develop Research Skills*. Minneapolis: Lerner Publications, 1990.

Miller, Elizabeth B. *The Internet Resource Directory for K-12 Teachers and Librarians*. Englewood: Libraries Unlimited, 1998.

Moen, Christine Boardman. *Better Than Book Reports*. New York: Scholastic, 1992.

Page, P. Elizabeth, Elaine Homestead, and Karen McGinnis. (1993). "Designing Rubrics for Authentic Assessment." *Middle School Journal*. 25, 25-27.

Sharan, Yael, and Shlomo Sharan. *Expanding Cooperative Learning Through Group Investigation*. New York: Teachers College Press, 1992.

Stahl, Robert J. (Editor). *Cooperative Learning in Social Studies*. Menlo Park: Addison-Wesley Publishing, 1994.

Stone, Jeanne. *Cooperative Learning Writing Activities*. San Juan Capistrano: Kagan Cooperative Learning, 1995.

Taggart, Germaine L., Sandra J. Phifer, Judy A. Nixon, and Marilyn Wood. *Rubrics: A Handbook for Construction and Use*. Lancaster: Technomic Publishing Company, Inc., 1998.

Vermette, Paul J. *Making Cooperative Learning Work: Student Teams in K-12 Classrooms*. New Jersey: Prentice-Hall, 1998.